DANGEROUS
LOVE

November 21, 16

Dear Jane

Thank you for helping me with the Bolthouse Investments info.

Ray's book is in a country where it's against the law to preach Christianity we are buddies. I hope you like it. Best regards. Sean

CONTENTS

"There is no circumstance, no trouble, no testing, that can ever touch me until, first of all, it has gone past God and past Christ, right through to me. If it has come that far, it has come with great purpose."

—ALAN REDPATH

For my parents, Bill and Lois Norman, who humbly taught me that seeking to follow God, and loving all people while doing so, results in the deepest satisfaction and greatest joys in life; and for my wife, Hélène, who has spent most of her life helping and showing me how to do just that.

Published in Nashville, Tennessee, by Nelson Books, an imprint of Thomas Nelson. Nelson Books and Thomas Nelson are registered trademarks of HarperCollins Christian Publishing, Inc.

Published in association with the William Denzel Agency, www.williamdenzel.com.

Thomas Nelson titles may be purchased in bulk for educational, business, fund-raising, or sales promotional use. For information, please e-mail SpecialMarkets@ThomasNelson.com.

ISBN 978-0-7180-7803-4 (IE)

Cataloging-in-Publication Data is on file with the Library of Congress.

ISBN 978-0-7180-2708-7

Printed in the United States of America

15 16 17 18 19 20 RRD 6 5 4 3 2

DANGEROUS
LOVE

A TRUE STORY OF TRAGEDY, FAITH, AND
———————— FORGIVENESS ————————
IN THE MUSLIM WORLD

RAY NORMAN

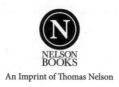

NELSON
BOOKS

An Imprint of Thomas Nelson

I knew my chances of survival were almost nil the moment I saw the gun—and the expressionless look in the eyes of the turbaned Arab who had stepped out of the sand dunes next to our stationary, four-wheel-drive vehicle. My panicked thoughts and exploding emotions quickly converged on the survival of my ten-year-old daughter, Hannah, cowering in the seat next to me. When the man turned his aim from my head toward her, something rose up within me that was more than just instinctive protest. "No! No! Not my daughter!"

When my wife and I first came to the isolated Islamic republic of Mauritania to work among the poor, we asked God to mold us and use our lives in whatever way he saw fit for the sake of those we knew he had called us to serve and love. Over the years multiple circumstances had caused me to carefully reassess the risks and be reconciled with the fact that this work I loved so much could well cost me my life. But surely that commitment did not include the life of our daughter!

The same instant I saw the man aim at Hannah, I threw myself against the window to block the shot and heard the dull, thundering report of the gun as it shattered our world. Glass went flying everywhere. I felt the numbing pain of the bullet as it ripped through my arm, and I heard Hannah's scream as she reacted to the chaos and horror of the moment. Before the gunman could take aim again, I slammed the idling car into gear and spun off just as he fired his remaining shots through the rear window into the back of my seat.

Once out of range of the gunman and thinking we were out of immediate danger, I turned to Hannah to comfort her and to see if *she had been wounded by the flying glass shards. But my mounting hope of survival quickly crumbled when I looked her way. Choking back the dark fear that was welling up within me, I reached across her bloodied seat to see why she was clutching the front of her dress. As I pulled my little girl's trembling hands away, I saw in the center of her heaving chest a deep, hollow, and jagged bullet hole—and flowing from it a steady, meandering stream of bright, crimson blood. It was then that my already shattered world fell completely apart.*

Alone and surrounded by only the blowing dunes of the western Sahara Desert—and hundreds of miles from any reliable emergency medical facilities—my mind and heart groped frantically for a remaining thread of hope. Everything in me pleaded for a small measure of reassurance, or even a divine injunction to the surreal events of the last five minutes from the One to whom I had committed my life and soul. In a dry, rasping whisper of desperation, I forced words of protest up from the depths of my heart and out into the hot, dusty, desert air: "No, no, dear Lord! This is not the way it was supposed to be! Not my daughter! Take my life, but give me my daughter!"

I knew my chances of survival were almost nil the moment I saw the gun—and the expressionless look in the eyes of the turbaned Arab who had stepped out of the sand dunes next to our stationary, four-wheel-drive vehicle. My panicked thoughts and exploding emotions quickly converged on the survival of my ten-year-old daughter, Hannah, cowering in the seat next to me. When the man turned his aim from my head toward her, something rose up within me that was more than just instinctive protest. "No! No! Not my daughter!"

When my wife and I first came to the isolated Islamic republic of Mauritania to work among the poor, we asked God to mold us and use our lives in whatever way he saw fit for the sake of those we knew he had called us to serve and love. Over the years multiple circumstances had caused me to carefully reassess the risks and be reconciled with the fact that this work I loved so much could well cost me my life. But surely that commitment did not include the life of our daughter!

The same instant I saw the man aim at Hannah, I threw myself against the window to block the shot and heard the dull, thundering report of the gun as it shattered our world. Glass went flying everywhere. I felt the numbing pain of the bullet as it ripped through my arm, and I heard Hannah's scream as she reacted to the chaos and horror of the moment. Before the gunman could take aim again, I slammed the idling car into gear and spun off just as he fired his remaining shots through the rear window into the back of my seat.

Once out of range of the gunman and thinking we were out of immediate danger, I turned to Hannah to comfort her and to see if *she had been wounded by the flying glass shards. But my mounting hope of survival quickly crumbled when I looked her way. Choking back the dark fear that was welling up within me, I reached across her bloodied seat to see why she was clutching the front of her dress. As I pulled my little girl's trembling hands away, I saw in the center of her heaving chest a deep, hollow, and jagged bullet hole—and flowing from it a steady, meandering stream of bright, crimson blood. It was then that my already shattered world fell completely apart.*

Alone and surrounded by only the blowing dunes of the western Sahara Desert—and hundreds of miles from any reliable emergency medical facilities—my mind and heart groped frantically for a remaining thread of hope. Everything in me pleaded for a small measure of reassurance, or even a divine injunction to the surreal events of the last five minutes from the One to whom I had committed my life and soul. In a dry, rasping whisper of desperation, I forced words of protest up from the depths of my heart and out into the hot, dusty, desert air: "No, no, dear Lord! This is not the way it was supposed to be! Not my daughter! Take my life, but give me my daughter!"

1

DESERT SOJOURNERS

I will praise you, Lord, among the nations;
I will sing of you among the peoples.
For great is your love.
(Psalm 57:9–10)

IT WAS ONE OF THOSE FIERCELY HOT DAYS ONLY THE WESTERN Sahara can dish out in May and June. The temperature was a stifling 110 degrees Fahrenheit by late morning, and the Saharan dust hung thickly in the air, limiting visibility through the Land Cruiser's windshield to less than two hundred yards. I was heading back to the office after visiting members of a microenterprise cooperative in a desperately poor settlement on the outskirts of Nouakchott, Mauritania. As I drove I had to negotiate the potholed remnants of one of the few paved thoroughfares in the town while dodging the odd donkey cart, a few heavily laden camels, and (far worse) several of the town's hundreds of dilapidated, honking taxis—manned by turban-clad drivers whose opportunities for practice driving must have paled in comparison to their more commonly acquired skills in camel riding. The occasional gust of wind caused the sand and litter in the streets to swirl, much like snow during a winter storm, but it brought no relief and felt more like the blast from a furnace than a natural breeze. On days such as this, the fine, red dust would penetrate and settle on every conceivable surface, through the best-sealed doors and windows and onto everything from the teacups in the kitchen cabinet to the toothbrush on the bathroom shelf. If I left the windows down in the Land Cruiser during the short drive to the office, I would arrive with a thin layer of dust coating my eyelids, and my hair would have a reddish-brown tint matching the desert landscape on the outskirts of town.

Nouakchott, the capitol of the Islamic Republic of Mauritania, was sprawled across the salt flats and undulating dunes that marked the thin, transitional line between the Sahara Desert to the east and the Atlantic to the west. In this teeming town of one million (nearly 40 percent of the country's population), half of the inhabitants were first-generation migrants who in recent years had reluctantly abandoned their failing pastoral livelihoods to the desert's southward encroachment and moved to the city in search of food and work. They occupied the expansive and ever-growing shantytowns that surrounded this old French-colonial outpost.

Mauritania, land of the Moors, is a little-known desert country in the Maghreb region of western North Africa, situated between Morocco to the north and Senegal and Mali to the south. On its western edge are two thousand kilometers of empty coastline where the great dunes of the Sahara Desert drop into the expanse of the Atlantic Ocean. The northern two-thirds of this arid land consist of endless dunes and rocky plateaus peppered with isolated oasis settlements, while the southern fringe falls into the marginally cultivable Sahel zone that borders the southern Sahara across Africa. The country is peopled by various ethnic groups steeped in their rich traditions and cultures: the dominant Arab-Berber Moors—a light-skinned and historically pastoralist people who speak a dialect of Arabic (Hassaniya)—and a number of minority black-African ethnic groups, mostly farmers who occupy largely the southern fringe.

In the Middle Ages, the area of modern-day Mauritania was part of the cradle of the Almoravid movement, which conquered and spread Islam throughout North Africa and into the southern half of Spain. As French-colonial interests spread across North and West Africa in the late 1800s, Mauritania eventually became a French protectorate, then gained its independence in 1960. In the years following its independence, the country experienced a series of conflicts with both Morocco and Senegal, several devastating droughts, and a succession of coups d'état that resulted in the establishment of military governments and somewhat authoritarian leadership. For most of its existence, Mauritania has largely depended on its drought-prone agriculture as well as coastal fishing and iron ore mining in remote desert outposts. In recent years it has been caught between seemingly competitive desires to preserve its traditions and deep Islamic heritage while engaging effectively with a rapidly modernizing and secular world—largely for the sake of improving the lives of its historically marginalized population.

Mauritania is a harsh land with rampant poverty. I thrived in this place, but for many development and humanitarian specialists working in Africa, this was one of those posts at the end of the line, a hardship post well known for its isolation and the plethora of challenges that came with it.

As I headed back to the office that day in 2001, my heart was filled with gratitude, and I seized the opportunity of a few solitary moments to reflect. In the midst of the heat and chaos of our daily lives, I was happy, deeply happy. With perhaps the exception of my childhood days spent romping through the rainforest behind my parents' missionary bungalow or cooling off in the river that ran in front of it, I could not recall another season in my life when I was so fulfilled. Hélène, my wife of French origin and a petite, unpretentious woman, was a loving and caring mother who had sacrificially accompanied me through six countries and across four continents as we sought to fulfill the calling on our lives. I had two happy, wonderful, and rambunctious children whose life experiences thus far had taught them that when it comes to laughter, fun, and intimate relationships, no boundaries need be set by color, race, culture, or even religious faith. I was right where my heart had called me to be: caring for my small family, serving among the world's poorest, loving my Muslim colleagues and neighbors, and trying to play a small part in making this hurting world a better place. Winding through the chaos of Nouakchott's streets that day, my feelings could best be articulated by Frederick Buechner's powerful words on vocation in his book *Wishful Thinking*: "The place God calls you to is the place where your deep gladness and the world's deep hunger meet." As I drove on, my thoughts wandered back over the journey that had brought us to this remote corner of the globe.

———◆———

American blood flows in my veins, but I was raised under the African sun, a sun that burned indelibly into my heart its sorrow and laughter, its fears and hopes, and its passions and beauty. One of three children of loving parents who worked as career missionaries, I was reared in the bush country of Nigeria and Ghana, where I reveled in the adventures and new horizons of each day and where much of my free time was spent roaming the tropical forest or the open hills that surrounded the mission stations.

When the sun was shining, as it often was, I was constantly outdoors—playing soccer with the village boys or joining them on a hunting trip in the nearby bush country or, best of all, joining them in my own dugout canoe for a fishing trip on the river that ran in front of our home in southeastern Nigeria. At an early age I was seized with the discomforting notion that life seemed a bit short if one were to adequately pursue all the adventures that it held—whether it was exploring the valley beyond the hills on the horizon or finding time to sit under a shade tree and listen to stories from a village elder about life in Africa "before the white men came." I packed my days full, trying to squeeze as many adventures as I could out of each moment.

During the long rainy season when tropical downpours could last for days at a stretch, I made sure that time was not wasted. The nearby river would flood its banks, transforming our yard into a veritable liquid playground. Usually my younger brother, Russell, my older sister, Jo Ellen, and I were out frolicking in our rain boots or paddling the washbasin around the deeper parts of the flooded yard like a cumbersome canoe. Such outings were followed by the ritual of pulling our boots and wet clothing off while checking each other meticulously for the many leeches that invariably attached themselves to us during our rambunctious play time.

If we weren't playing outside, we would spend endless hours entertaining ourselves indoors in inventive ways: building forts and castles with furniture and sheets, dressing up in our parents' clothes, devising complex games of hide-and-seek, or just sitting on the porch watching the huge tropical trees of the rainforest bend and wave under the wind and rain while we munched freshly roasted peanuts and told stories to one another.

Since much of my youth was spent in rural areas without television, comic books, or peer-induced perceptions of heroes, my admiration was often focused in those formative years on my missionary-doctor father. After homeschool or on Saturdays, I would often join him in his small clinic and watch him patiently and lovingly tend to the needs of multitudes of sick and hurting people, many of whom had never been to a doctor, much less had a personal encounter with a white man. He was often called in the middle of the night to help a village woman with a breech-position birth or to try to save the life of a fevered child with advanced malaria.

The eyes and heart of a child are perhaps the most discerning when it comes to matters of true affection, and I well remember at that young age being deeply aware of the genuineness of Dad's love for the people he felt called to serve. But it was only years later that I really began to understand the source of that love.

One of the more formative memories I have of my father is of the morning after he had been brutally attacked in the night by thugs seeking to rob the coffers of the small bush hospital in northern Ghana. He had been beaten, stripped of his clothing, and left tied to a barbed wire fence a few miles out from the village. Early the next morning, with blood still seeping through the bandages on his arms, back, and head, he came to my room and gently explained what had happened. It was already a chaotic morning, but sensing that I needed some time with him, he asked me to join him on an errand in the village. As we drove he explained that one of the bandits had been caught, and Dad had been asked to come to the jail to identify him.

As we approached the small jailhouse, we were shocked to see it surrounded by a large, angry mob—some brandishing sticks and machetes—calling for immediate justice against the man who had attacked their doctor and put the hospital at risk. They quickly quieted as Dad and I worked our way through the crowd to the jail. Dad asked the policemen if we could have a few minutes alone with the assailant, and the moments that followed are forever etched in my memory.

In that small jail cell we found a trembling, frightened, and already badly beaten man. As the crowd jeered outside, he begged Dad for help. Dad sat with him, attempted to learn something about him with a few questions, and gently tried to calm his fears. The man claimed to have a Christian background, so Dad read to him a few assuring passages of hope from a small New Testament, and he prayed with the prisoner and gave him the copy of the Scriptures from which he had read. As we left he urged the policemen to do all in their power to protect the prisoner and beseeched the crowd to let things be and return to their homes.

Dad always demonstrated to his children that justice does not have to preclude mercy and compassion. But on that day I saw this principle extended well beyond familiar boundaries. It slowly dawned on me that I did not have sole, privileged access to Dad's mercy. In spite of the gravity of the sin, and the personal harm inflicted on my father, Dad demonstrated (to the prisoner—and to me and those around us) that the man who had attacked him was still a person of value both to Dad and to God, and worthy of receiving some measure of mercy and hope in spite of his self-inflicted circumstances.

During those years at the missionary stations, we lived primarily on local food, and we ate well. Our diet most commonly consisted of fresh fish caught in the nearby river, prepared in a delicious traditional stew of red palm oil and okra, and served up with local yams. One morning, however, when I was still quite young, my mother surprised us with a jar of purple grape jelly she had hidden away since our last trip to the United States. She had baked fresh bread, and as we sat down to breakfast, she warned me not to let my eyes get bigger than my stomach and end up wasting our precious jar of American jelly. I was halfway through my third piece of jellied toast when I realized I should have heeded her wise words. I couldn't finish that last piece.

Later that day when I was playing alone outside, I heard an unfamiliar noise near an old barrel in which we placed garbage for composting. I slipped behind a nearby tree, and as I peered around I recognized the young woman whose back was turned to me—a physically and mentally disabled woman I had often seen begging in the nearby village. Dressed in rags and holding an infant in one arm, she quietly rummaged through the garbage until her eyes obviously fixed on something. She reached far down into the barrel and gingerly withdrew her prize—my half-eaten piece of toast with that wonderful, purple jelly spread across its surface. I remember watching in stunned silence as she carefully removed specks of trash stuck to the jellied toast and ever so tenderly began to break off small bits and feed them to her child.

This experience, and many similar ones that followed in the ensuing years, instilled in me at a young age that all was not well in this world. I was certainly struck by how good my lot in life was compared to many around me, but it was also at this early age that I first remember notions of service and vocational calling tumbling around in my head and heart—and the birth of a desire to do something with my life that would help make the world a little better place for those such as that woman and her tiny infant.

After returning to the States around the age of fifteen, I experienced the typical challenges of disillusionment and isolation felt by most "third culture kids." I had spent my developmental years largely outside the culture of my parents and was adept at crafting relationships in most cultural milieus. But I never fully owned any one culture, including those of my parents. I recoiled at the confines of suburban American life and longed for the freedom of the open savanna plains and tropical forests of my earlier youth, as well as the relative simplicity of life and relationships in rural Africa. I did not fit in with my American peers, and to me their outlooks seemed shallow, short-sighted, and dominated by ethnocentric and materialistic notions.

What surprised and confused me more was that the same shallow and self-focused outlook on one's purpose in life seemed to also pervade some of those who populated the churches we associated with; any claim God had on their lives may have included certain duties on Sunday and an occasional pull on their purses and billfolds, but I was often surprised when I encountered church people who seemed to possess little notion of sacrifice and laying oneself down for the sake of others. In some of the churches we intersected with—many of them housed in magnificent edifices—coming together seemed to be more of a social event than a gathering of people who sought to encounter the God they served. This was all new and foreign to me, as much of my church experience to this point had been humble and sincere gatherings under a village shade tree. What little I knew of Scripture and what I saw in many American churches did not add up, and I passed through a season in which I was disillusioned and bitter. With time, however, I was able to stop mourning the past. I found that simply focusing on the potential of the future resulted in brighter mornings and increasingly more hope-filled days.

By my late teens I had begun to wrestle with the claim God had on my own life, an exercise replete with thorny issues and considerably more discomforting than sorting out his claim on my Christian compatriots. A clearer sense of calling to work among the poor and unreached began to form in my own heart. I wanted to lay down my life in service to those in need, but I was still uncomfortable with the idea of stepping completely out of my comfort zone. More specifically, I had dreams of perhaps pursuing theological studies and then spending my years of service in a wild, beautiful setting with just a few creature comforts. After completing a day of good works, my evening would be spent watching herds of passing wildebeests silhouetted by the dazzling African sunset and framed by surrounding mountains. I never imagined myself in a blazing hot and dusty corner of some remote desert outpost.

This was my alabaster jar of sorts, something I knew I would eventually have to break to let the contents flow out, hopefully somewhere near the foot of the cross. Moreover, I wrestled not only with what I might have to give up but also with what I knew I lacked. Having been raised in Africa by missionary parents, I had some understanding of the cost of such a commitment. I had watched them live through the challenges of loneliness, isolation, exhaustion, disease, and civil war; and I knew that obedience to God's call, while deeply satisfying, could also be costly. But I also knew that to effectively touch the lives of those you are called to serve, you have to possess a genuine love. I wanted to serve him anywhere and with any people he might lead me to, but I also knew that many of the most unreached, broken, and hurting communities in our world are found among people who follow Islam—this was especially true for those parts of the world I had been privileged to be acquainted with up to this time in my life. Yet in spite of their overwhelming physical needs, I had little attraction to Muslim people, much less any real love. And this was my dilemma: I wanted to serve him in the neediest parts of the world, but how can you serve a people when you are deficient in the very thing that provides strength in your weakness and brings life to your service? So it was here that my journey truly began. I had genuinely counted the cost and told God I would serve him wherever he led. I could probably manage to pour out the contents of my alabaster jar, but he would have to work a love into my heart that was not my own.

As college days loomed on the horizon, I had a strong personal interest and thirst to know Scripture better, and I seriously contemplated theological studies, as many young people who want to serve abroad do these days. But having grown up with the poor, I knew what kept them awake at night were the hunger-induced wails of their children, not the condition of their souls—and that Scripture is better lived out than taught, at least initially. So, pouring a little bit more of my dreams out of that alabaster jar, I set my intellectual sights elsewhere and soon found myself captivated by studies in agriculture and water resources engineering—a source of skills that would open wonderful doors of opportunity to both learn and serve in the years ahead. A few years later I found myself in the Niger Republic, situated in the dry Sahel region of West Africa and at that time the poorest country in the world, studying irrigation systems and collecting water data for my doctoral thesis.

It was there that I met my future wife and life partner, Hélène, a petite European of French nationality and a short-term missionary with the Sudan Interior Mission (SIM). (SIM was originally founded as a missions agency to work among people in the tropical savanna region of West Africa. Today it works around the world as the International Mission Society while still retaining the acronym SIM.) I was living alone in a small town some nine hours out of the capital city, Niamey, and made the long, dusty drive in for supplies every few weeks. On one of these trips to Niamey I got caught in midday traffic, stuck in the stifling heat between a donkey cart and a broken-down truck. Hot, frustrated, and dreaming of finding a cool spot somewhere for a siesta, I heard a moped (a small, motorized bike) come puttering up from behind. Forcing myself out of a heat-induced daze, I watched in utter amazement as the moped's owner gingerly wove in and out of the traffic and the sea of pedestrians, passed my jeep, and wound on past the traffic jam. A helmet and clothing were all I could see of the driver at first— that and a pair of well-tanned Caucasian legs sticking out from under a modest skirt and perched on the moped so as to avoid the spewing hot motor oil and the filth of the streets.

Perhaps I had spent too many days in the desert sun, but as she waved at me before disappearing around the broken truck in front of me in a puff of dust, I found myself wheeling the little jeep out of the line of traffic, parting the pedestrians rushing to the local marketplace, and traversing the front courtyards of a few roadside stores to give pursuit. I had recognized her as someone I had encountered all too briefly at a small church meeting in the city some weeks before but really knew little about her except that she avoided the expatriate crowd, preferring the company of Nigeriens. I had no idea where she was headed, but when I pulled up behind her at the front gate of her home, she was obviously perplexed and a little cautious to find that a relative stranger had followed her there.

I was clearly off to a rocky start, but in the months that followed, the more I learned of her, the more I was drawn to her. Being the reasonable person she was, she was doubtful at first; but after many exchanged letters, a few expensive phone calls, and four agonizingly slow months, we became engaged.

Hélène, the daughter of a French father and an English mother, was raised in France and studied in England and Germany. While studying in Heidelberg, Germany, she became friends with a young woman involved with an evangelical pietist community who lovingly and gently introduced Hélène to Christ. Before leaving Germany, she was asked to assist as an English-German translator at a major missions conference in Switzerland, and while she listened to reports from around the world, a love for nations and peoples beyond her own familiar European communities grew in her heart. Returning to London to finish her course of studies, she spent a year working for the British and Foreign Bible Society before joining SIM as a one-year volunteer to Niger.

Hélène had suffered through periods of deep pain and brokenness in some of her childhood and teenage years—experiences with which I was largely unfamiliar. But I soon learned that those who have traversed such valleys in their lives have a unique ability to distinguish between the things in life that are truly important and the things that are not. In the years ahead, her discernment played an important role in shaping her life and our family's, as well as the choices we made at important intersections in our lives.

In 1985 we were married in Niamey at a simple service in the home of friends. The small wedding was attended by a few of our American, European, and Nigerian acquaintances. I remember how privileged I felt when one of our street friends (a crippled beggar) came crawling in on all fours, greeted us with a big, toothy grin, and happily climbed into one of the guest chairs just as the wedding march was being forced out of the portable (and expiring) electric organ. At the reception that followed, wedding guests were served rice with local stew and their choice of a lukewarm soft drink. It was the grandest wedding I have ever attended. Three days later we loaded the small jeep with our meager belongings, and with our hearts fixed on David's words from Psalm 57:9–10, we turned out of town toward the desert and headed down the long dusty road to our future: "I will praise you, Lord, among the nations; I will sing of you among the peoples. For great is your love . . ."

For the next fifteen years my wife and I were planted among Muslim communities in Africa and the Middle East, usually working among the poor. After six years in Niger, our journey took us to the Sultanate of Oman, Côte d'Ivoire, and Egypt before we landed in Mauritania. Our experiences in each country and with each people shaped us in unique ways. Overall, there was a gradual but major shift in the way we understood those we hoped to serve. But parallel to this was an equally important, and perhaps more necessary, shift in the way we understood ourselves—as God slowly peeled away layers of cultural ignorance, spiritual arrogance, and prejudice in our lives that hindered the ready flow of Christ's passion for all peoples.

Our journey, especially in the early years, was full of soul-searching lessons as we tried to reach across the cultural divides we encountered. As with others who come out of the enclaves of Western culture, we were used to never having to take a step from the comfort or security of our customary environments. But we soon found that effective living and learning in today's global and pluralistic society require effort. It takes time—and it comes at a personal cost. It requires being deliberate about moving out of our comfort zones, placing ourselves in often vulnerable positions, and actively engaging across cultures.

Not everyone will accept you right off; not everyone is going to understand or appreciate your efforts. There will be setbacks and even failures. But we found that persistence, mixed with humility and grace, pay off in the end, and the rewards are usually multiples of what you invest.

But there were more painful lessons we encountered on a deeper level. Beyond the realm of honest blunders, we found ourselves increasingly encountering our own weaknesses, our own shortcomings—fractures, as it were, in what we thought were solid emotional and spiritual foundations in our own lives. When these weaknesses showed through the surface of our work and ministry, they plunged us into seasons of disappointment, self-doubt, and discouragement.

This happened when we first arrived in the small, mountainous country of Oman, beautifully nestled along the turquoise-blue shores of the Arabian Peninsula and populated by a gentle people steeped in their Islamic traditions. In spite of the sincerity of our efforts, we blundered foolishly with a number of newfound acquaintances who reached out to us in genuine friendship. Whether it was in our enthusiasm and haste to share our faith, rather than first investing in the crafting of caring relationships, or the articulation of ill-informed comments about the Islamic faith, we quickly found that our actions were often unnecessarily offensive and hurtful. Our mistakes brought on by our shallow forethought caused us to examine our own hearts more carefully. Were we more concerned about the well-being of others, or seeing the tangible and timely fruit of our labors? Was our trust truly in

God, in his timing and in his ways, or was it in our own ability to reason and convince?

We knew God loves all people fully and unconditionally, but we recognized a temptation to dominate and control others with our personal beliefs and perceptions. And we also recognized that this flowed from our fear of weakness, our own insecurities, and the fragility of our own understanding of God and his ways. We began to see that initial inroads into the hearts of Muslims are perhaps best made through life and deed, rather than word. We also learned to relax and be more transparent in our relationships. With time—and in spite of our deficiencies—we were able to touch people's lives and to see genuine fruit from our labors. The diagnostics we made on our hearts humbled us. We knew we were still apprentice workers in the vineyard and did not have all the answers. But the experience was an invaluable crash course in better understanding Peter's admonition that, in sharing the hope that is within us, we must do so "with gentleness and respect" (1 Peter 3:15).

Our early years in Africa and the Middle East also taught us that we did not always have the answers for the dire physical and spiritual needs of those around us—the crushing poverty and heart-rending spiritual bondage we encountered each day. But slowly, ever so slowly, we learned that hardly anyone turns away an act of kindness, a shared laugh, or even a shared tear. We began to see that effective loving does not require having all the immediate solutions for the challenges facing those we serve, or even for ourselves. We did not have to come in with a fixed plan or strategy; rather, we needed to simply and genuinely seek to love and value those we encountered. And with time we began to view our painful lessons as much-needed reminders of our own brokenness, our own need of repair, our own need of reconciled relationship—the very needs we were trying to help meet in others. We were slowly learning that for this work, God was far more interested in yielded vessels than perfect ones, and that pursuing a yielded heart is wholly different than pursuing perfection.

And then there was the most important lesson of all that slowly grew in our hearts with the seasoning of the years spent among people not our own. Simple as it may seem, it was the realization that in ourselves we did not have the capacity to love sufficiently. We saw that the limits of our love fell far short of the needs of those around us. But the more we offered ourselves as yielded vessels, the more we would begin to experience love flow though us that was clearly not of our making. We found that becoming acquainted with God's love for those he called us to serve is far more deeply satisfying than wrestling with the limits of our own love. This is the love that the world needs: his love for the people he gave his life for, a powerful love for which we are only vessels, a love that flows from our innermost parts, but whose source is beyond ourselves.

———◆———

As I pulled into a parking place under the large acacia tree that shaded the front of our office building, my thoughts were joggled out of the past and back to the very real present. I noticed that the modest orange-and-white sign indicating Mauritania's World Vision offices was covered with a greater than usual coat of dust on this stifling morning, but the logo's star of hope was a quiet and reassuring reminder of why I was in Mauritania. In this isolated Islamic republic, where Christian presence is restricted and open witness prohibited, World Vision serves as an advocate for the country's many poor communities and as a welcomed partner with the government in its efforts to combat rampant poverty. I was into my third year as national director of this strategic program, which continued to exist largely as a result of much prayer and the visionary leadership of those who had preceded me.

Again I reflected on how grateful I was to be in Mauritania with my family and for the opportunities and lessons along the way that had led us to this place. When Hélène and I first chose to follow God on this journey among the nations, we made the conscious decision to count the cost, take up our crosses, and follow. We both believed that there is no country too far that personal sacrifice could not (or should not) be made for the sake of those who suffer and live with little or no hope.

But counting the cost, in this sense, did not mean we had some window into the future. We could only see the cross, and we were compelled to look no further. We understood this. But we found our strength in the wonderful promise that wherever we were led, even to the ends of the earth, we would find Christ there. And we did, when we came to Mauritania. We experienced Christ's presence on the first day we set foot in that land; we saw him working through the lives of our coworkers; and we felt the tangible power of his love for the poor as we lived and worked among them. Sitting there in the Land Cruiser on that hot, dusty morning, I never could have anticipated the life-changing events that were about to unfold in our ministry among the poor or in the life of each member of our family. But I was conscious that morning of a deep assurance that whatever tomorrow held or wherever our journey led us, Christ too would be there.

---------- 2 ----------

TOWERS FALL IN THE SAHARA

What do you have against me that you
have attacked my country?
(JUDGES 11:12)

AMRITA, MY ADMINISTRATIVE ASSISTANT, STUCK HER HEAD THROUGH the doorway to say I had an urgent call from my wife. It was Tuesday, September 11, 2001. "I've just gotten off the phone with the American school," Hélène said, "and the American embassy has alerted them that it appears the Pentagon has been bombed."

I was in my office with Brian McCully, a seasoned World Vision staffer from New Zealand who had held a number of senior posts in the organization before going into semiretirement. We had met in Los Angeles some months before, and he had kindly offered to work with me in a mentoring relationship, something I welcomed in my rather lonely outpost. He had been in Nouakchott for several days, shadowing me as I worked and spending a couple of hours each day debriefing, counseling, advising. With nearly twenty-five years separating us, there were times we engaged in somewhat differing views—especially with respect to aspects of leadership needed for the complex challenges we faced as an institution rapidly moving into the second millennium. But he carried a wealth of knowledge and lessons learned from years of watching World Vision grow from its infancy, and I readily absorbed all he had to share about relationship-building, prioritization, team leadership and care, and (what I was wrestling with most at that time) balancing family and work while serving in areas of heart-wrenching human need, where new crises and challenges roll in before the previous ones are resolved.

I went to my computer, and in a few seconds the first images of smoke billowing from the towers of the World Trade Center appeared on the screen. Brian and I stared in stunned silence, slowly absorbing the impact of this event as it reverberated from New York City and Washington, DC, across the world, and even to this remote desert outpost. As I took it all in, I was shocked but not surprised at the events. Brian seemed clearly more surprised than I was. Perhaps he was less acquainted with the simmering frustration in much of the Muslim world with, among other things, what many perceived as growing interventionism from wealthy Western nations and the feeling of impotence to do anything about the global export of Western values and culture that they found both reprehensible and threatening. I quickly phoned several of our local senior expatriate staff to tell them about the events, including Myles Harrison, our security officer and the director of our large urban program in Nouakchott. After asking Amrita to track closely with the American embassy for any further announcements or warnings, I then took a few minutes to call Stan and Beth Doerr, an American couple who worked out of our regional office in Kiffa, some seven hundred kilometers inland.

The events in the United States were still ongoing at that point, and I knew I needed to monitor the news closely as things unfolded. During her phone call Hélène had reminded me that a recent sandstorm had taken out our television dish and that she had no access to CNN—one of the few accessible news networks in this area. Brian had an appointment with another staff member, so I headed home, stopping by a small television repair shop to see if I could get the owner to come to my house with me and repair our dish system within the hour for double his fee. My motivational negotiation worked. After a few minutes on our flat rooftop, he had the dish working. The images of the Pentagon and twin towers were soon on our home screen. By this time the second tower was down, and the connections between the events and Al-Qaeda were beginning to trickle in.

After fifteen minutes of listening to the news, Hélène turned to me and said, "Do you realize what this means, Ray? You are the director of the largest, openly Christian, humanitarian organization in the country. What's more, you are an American and this is an Islamic republic." I sat there silently absorbing the weight of Hélène's words. A few moments later she continued, "And do you understand the spiritual forces that must be at work in all of this? Surely we will not get through this unscathed."

I simply mumbled, "Oh, we don't need to worry about this now and jump to conclusions. We will simply watch and see how things play out. I am sure it will all be all right in the end." Hélène had lived with me long enough to know that it would be pointless to try to reason with me further.

Over the next few days, tight security measures were put in place in Nouakchott as news of the extent of the 9/11 causalities filtered in and the connection with Al-Qaeda became clear. The government put armed guards at our offices; military tanks were placed in front of the small American school Hannah attended and in front of the adjacent American embassy. Twenty-four-hour guardians were also stationed at our home. Embassy personnel and our own World Vision International security unit advised us to limit our movements to home, the office, and school—and to completely avoid public venues.

On the morning of September 12, as I walked into the office reception area on the first floor, I was surprised to see it nearly full and to find Amrita obviously flustered with all the phone calls she had already received in the first few minutes of the workday. Beginning that morning, and continuing for the next three days, we were overwhelmed with visitors and phone calls from Mauritanians from all walks of life—government personnel, civic leaders, business clients, neighbors, and friends—all coming to offer their condolences and expressions of sorrow, some of them in tears, for what had happened in the United States on 9/11 by the hands of fellow Muslims. I was amazed and deeply touched by the warmth and sincerity of so many of our Mauritanian friends and colleagues, many of whom seemed to be as disturbed and traumatized as any American was. Time and again I heard the words, "Please don't associate these acts with all of us [Muslims]. What you have seen and witnessed does not represent the feelings and views of most Muslim people!"

In the ensuing days we learned that one of the senior Al-Qaeda operatives working with Bin Laden had some past connection with Mauritania, although he no longer lived there. A short time later he appeared as number four on the list of top Al-Qaeda terrorists listed by President George W. Bush's administration. This did not help matters as far as local political and ideological tensions were concerned. There were pockets of sympathy in Mauritania for the perpetuators of 9/11, but they were clearly a minority. Each day the local papers expressed a wide range of viewpoints on these matters. When word got out a few days later that the United States was considering an invasion of Afghanistan, this only added to the already heightened tensions we were sensing. All Americans in the country were encouraged to exercise continued caution, and a communiqué was sent out to all American Peace Corp volunteers stationed in various parts of the country to report back to Nouakchott for a security briefing.

About this time officials from the American embassy called an afternoon briefing for all American citizens in Nouakchott. The ambassador, recently assigned to Mauritania and a man whom I admired greatly, was traveling abroad at the time, so his deputies were in charge of the meeting. I was a little surprised that the tone of the meeting downplayed the state of affairs, with just a general admonition to avoid areas where students might be protesting and an attitude that conveyed that things would probably settle down in a few days. I was particularly concerned with how out of touch some of the American officials seemed to be with events going on around town. I had the advantage of a staff deeply engaged on a daily basis with the communities we served, including some 150 dedicated Mauritanians who helped us keep our ears to the ground. They painted a more cautious picture. During the briefing I remember asking embassy personnel what they thought about the presence of the Taliban mosque in a certain quarter of town—a fairly small operation recently started by a handful of Taliban who had a following of about seventy people. This was a situation my staff had kept me apprised of for some time, as we had a number of projects in the same area of town. To my surprise the embassy staff admitted they had no knowledge of such a group. While many of us at World Vision (both expatriate and Mauritanian) knew things were more unsettled than appearances let on, we felt that our long experience in the communities—and the trust we had built with them—allowed us to reasonably negotiate the troubled terrain we were facing. I was not sure some of my fellow Americans were as well prepared. So, I proffered that, while I, too, believed there was no reason for alarm, the atmosphere around town was probably more unsettled (and potentially combustible) than they might think; at least that was the view of my staff. They thanked me for my input, and the meeting soon came to a close, with many of us wondering why we had all been assembled if there were no significant threats.

In my years of relating to embassy officials, I had certainly met those who were seasoned diplomats, men and women who took seriously their mandate to effectively and appropriately represent their country in a foreign land, diplomats who were not only practiced and skilled at relating across cultural divides but who also deeply valued the importance of such skill sets. But there were times I was dismayed by the attitudes and behavior of some embassy staff who seemed to lack a depth of understanding and appreciation of the cultural milieu. Too often I observed comportment that was aloof and oozed a sense of entitlement relative to the people and the local conditions where they were posted, and I sensed many failed to understand that respect from local citizens was something we all needed to earn, not expect. These were individuals who represented my country and its people in foreign lands. But with all the investment our government puts into its foreign service, I often wondered why they were not more effectively prepared for their strategic roles in an ever-shrinking world where cultural competence is in increasing demand.

In addition to some of our senior staff at World Vision, there was a scattering of other expatriate Protestant Christians (primarily from other African nations, Latin America, the United States, and Europe) working under various auspices (usually small humanitarian outfits) who assembled on Fridays at facilities provided by the local Catholic church. This was the only non-Muslim religious infrastructure in Nouakchott. It had been present since pre-independence days and was the only legally sanctioned church entity in the country, exclusively serving the small expatriate community. Mauritanians were strictly forbidden to participate in any activities held there.

I had a great admiration for the French priests who ran the church, as they had dealt with periods of challenge and even persecution. A number of years earlier, one of them had lost an arm when he was attacked on the church grounds by an unstable, machete-wielding Muslim radical. Remarkably, this priest continued his service in Mauritania for a number of years afterward. Over the years these French priests had graciously allowed the expatriate Protestant community to use their facilities for a weekly service held on Fridays, the first day of the country's official weekend and the Muslim weekly day of prayer. They also shared their facilities for other small meetings during the week, such as the women's monthly prayer meeting that Hélène often attended.

Once a month or so a number of us from this larger gathering would gather in someone's home simply to encourage one another and to pray for Mauritania and its people. During the Gulf War a few years earlier, many of these people and their organizations (including World Vision) had shut down operations for a season due to security concerns since the Mauritanian administration at that time was in support of Saddam Hussein's offensive in Kuwait. This informal group called a special meeting to confer and pray about how we, as Christians working in the country, should react and respond to this new set of circumstances. A number of these people had young families and were torn between their own safety and their sense of calling to work alongside the people of Mauritania. We met for two consecutive nights, some of us fasting during the preceding days, conferring and then praying long into the night to seek guidance and direction. I had a tendency in such meetings not to say much but to listen, observe, and try to get a sense of how God was working among my colleagues.

I am not one who is given to frequent dreams and visions. But toward the end of the second evening, as most of us were kneeling in various parts of the living room quietly seeking God's direction, a clear scene began opening up before me (whether in my mind's eye or in my spirit, I am not sure). The image was a remote place in the Mauritanian desert. Each person in that evening's gathering was there. But we were each bare, completely naked, standing upright although buried in the sand up to our thighs or waists and scattered together among the dunes. My first impression was that we were all in an extremely vulnerable situation—dangerously exposed to a blazing sun and the raw, harsh elements of the remote desert and without any source of water or nourishment. We were all standing there, half buried in the sand, when we began quietly and gently singing songs of Scripture and hope. Soon our singing intensified, and it was focused on the nation we were in. In a few moments we were all singing petitions to God for his outpouring of mercy and grace on this land. We had forgotten about our extreme vulnerability in the blazing hot sand and were solely focused on our song of intercession. As we continued I began to notice a Mauritanian or two in the distance, mounted on their camels, who turned and began to approach us out of curiosity. Others began approaching on foot, and in a short time there was a large gathering of Mauritanian people around us watching intently as we sang. Soon one of them began singing along with us, then another and another until the entire gathering was singing in unison songs of petition for God's outpouring on the land. Then I began to hear drops of rain, slowly at first, and as I looked toward the sky, I saw the approaching thunderclouds rolling in. As we all continued to sing with a strong, united voice, rain began to fall with an intensity I had never seen before in this country.

That is the vision I saw.

Some thirty minutes later our time of prayer began to come to an end. We each took some time to go around the room and share what we had sensed during the prayer time to see if there was a general consensus on the direction in which God might be leading us as a group. I was still pondering what I had seen, uncomfortable with the notion of sharing it for fear others would think it strange. When my turn came to add my thoughts, I stumbled around for words at first, but then decided to just come out with it. I shared openly, although a bit reticently, all I had seen, cringing inwardly that others (especially those on my staff) would think me over the top or trying to sensationalize our circumstances. I was particularly concerned about the potential reaction of one of my senior staff, whose discomfort with some of my directives and general style of leadership had caused some tension in our relationship— although he was a capable person in his own right. To my surprise the entire room listened attentively and with evident interest.

When I finished the room was quiet at first. Then, much to my astonishment, one by one, people in the room thanked me sincerely for sharing my vision. After some continued discussion we each came away from that meeting with the deep conviction that we should maintain our programs and continue the work each of us was doing. We did not leave that meeting feeling any safer or more assured of our security, but we did come away with the belief that we should stay. As we dispersed Stan and Beth Doerr, along with others, warmly assured me that this was exactly what they too had felt about our continued presence in Mauritania. And then, to my astonishment, my colleague with whom I had had some tension came up to me and shared how deeply he was impacted by my words, adding, "When I heard you share what you had both seen and sensed, I said to myself, *This is the type of leader I can follow.*" I was dumbfounded but grateful for his unexpected words.

By early October things seemed to begin settling back toward normal in Nouakchott, and we were grateful to begin focusing our energies once again on our work, specifically the well-being of the communities, and especially the children, we were there to serve.

Then on October 7, 2001, the United States began its assault on Afghanistan, and things once again took a tense turn. Immediately there was a surge of anti-American rhetoric on the local radio, in local papers, and at mosques around the country. Many who had strongly condemned the acts of 9/11 and who had no sympathy for Al-Qaeda or its goals felt uncomfortable with the American entry into Afghanistan. The next day students began organizing anti-American marches in several areas of Nouakchott. Some of our drivers and staff began reporting having stones thrown at World Vision vehicles in specific parts of the town, so we removed the large World Vision logos from our fleet.

Early on the morning of October 8, I received an urgent call from Stan Doerr in Kiffa. A boisterous and fun-loving North Dakotan who had a teddy bear's heart, Stan was the director of our Assaba People's Program (named after the expansive desert region where the various projects were located). His quiet wife, Beth, a gardener par-excellence from Georgia who had a knack for making the desert bloom, oversaw our agricultural work. A note written in Arabic and addressed to the Doerrs had been left overnight on the front gate of our World Vision office in Kiffa. It addressed the Doerrs as monkeys and dogs, declared jihad against them, and warned them that their lives were in danger if they did not leave.

I conferred with Myles Harrison and our international security office in the United States. In the meantime Stan had a meeting with the provincial governor in Kiffa, who was an ardent advocate for World Vision and its work in his province. He assured Stan that he would find the note's authors, pull out all stops to ensure Stan and Beth's safety, and urged them not to let this interrupt World Vision's work in the region. Within a few hours policemen were stationed at their home and the World Vision office.

I asked Stan if he and Beth would feel better if they came to Nouakchott until things settled down, but they both spoke of the overwhelming love and support they felt from their Mauritanian neighbors and the local authorities, and I remember Beth saying she did not want to leave where she felt called to be simply out of fear. As long as there was reasoned assurance and confidence on the part of friends and colleagues in the local community that they would be safe, she wanted to stay. I told them I would leave the decision to them, and they eagerly (and courageously) chose to stay put.

Given the backlash from America's invasion of Afghanistan,

along with the incident with the Doerrs and a few other similar incidents in the country, the Peace Corps made the decision to pull out its one-hundred-plus volunteers stationed across the country. This was a huge disappointment for the Mauritanian government, which wanted to continue its growing relationship with the United States and maintain a wholesome public face to the rest of the world, in spite of the present unrest. During the week following this decision, Stan and Beth unselfishly helped a number of volunteers move safely from their up-country posts to the capital. The Peace Corps volunteers were given the choice of reassignment to another country or early leave.

In my interactions with people in the communities where we worked, opinions differed about America's actions in Afghanistan. Some people supported it while others strongly disagreed, but most simply kept their thoughts to themselves and went about their daily affairs. A more revealing reaction I encountered from time to time was a sense of insecurity and genuine fear regarding America's actions. On several occasions (especially during personal conversations with community friends and usually when talking with village women and mothers) I was asked, "Do you think Bush (or the Americans) will bomb us next, once they are finished with Afghanistan?" Many sincerely thought that President Bush was on a global vendetta to punish all Muslim countries for the acts of 9/11, and such questions were painful and heart-rending for me to hear. There was also a fair amount of rhetoric coming through United States media channels—poorly written articles or poorly articulated discussions on radio or television, in which Muslims and Islam were referred to, in whole, as a global threat or "the enemy," without distinguishing the radical fringe that was responsible for the recent acts of terrorism.

Another question that was confidentially posed to me on occasion was, "Why do Americans hate us [Muslims] so much? Do they not understand that we are not all the same nor do we hold to the same ideologies? Why is this so hard for well-educated Americans to understand?" I could not really speak for my fellow Americans. I felt disheartened by things I had heard, even in the Christian media. So many Muslims around the world were traumatized, hurting, confused, and vulnerable as a consequence of all that was happening and being said around the world. If there was ever a time for the church, especially in America, to reach out with understanding and loving compassion, it was now. But such insight and wisdom on behalf of most of our churches back home was not to be. And I, for one, sincerely believe the church missed out on one of its greatest opportunities in recent history to touch the Muslim world in a significant way.

And then there is the issue of poverty in the Muslim world, which many Americans do not seem to understand. For many of us living and working in majority Muslim countries, the events of 9/11 were shocking and heart-rending, but not entirely surprising. My World Vision colleagues and I were well aware that we live in a world of increasing economic, cultural, and political disparities. The gulf between the rich and poor is greater than ever before in human history, and most Muslims in the world today are poor.

Hélène and I first experienced the breadth of these disparities in our years in Niger, and most notably during the drought and famine of 1985. Niger is a harsh and challenging country in all respects (physically, socially, and spiritually), and today this largely Muslim nation remains one of the poorest countries in the world according to United Nation figures. It was in Niger that we encountered poverty as we had never before seen it. We learned the sobering truth that poverty is not just a distant problem, a systemic issue of a few dysfunctional states, or the result of a major environmental disaster or a lazy, unmotivated population.

In its purest form poverty has a face and a name—such as Salamatou, our crippled neighbor, who was reduced to begging after losing her husband and who never knew from one day to the next where she would find tomorrow's meal for her three small children; or Miriam, a fourteen-year-old Touareg girl who weighed less than sixty pounds and was brought to our home at six o'clock one morning by her father because he knew nowhere else to turn as she lay dying in his arms from malnutrition and dysentery; or Mohammed, a farmer with whom I worked, who would gaze out over his drought-ravaged crops knowing that several in his family would not survive through the next season; or the displaced Bouzou women camped in the dunes near our home who, because they were too malnourished to produce their own milk, would dig up handfuls of clay from our driveway, mix the clay with water, and feed it to their babies to quell their crying through the false sense of a full stomach. These were our friends and neighbors, those whom we wanted to serve and bring hope. But how do you have fellowship with and enter into the lives of those who live on less than a dollar a day? Their hope extended only to the next day, to perhaps the next meal or handout; our hopes extended into the years and decades ahead, college for the kids, retirement, and certainly to the hamburger or pizza we would eat when we next journeyed into the city.

These were painfully hard times for us as we struggled to understand how to demonstrate Christ's love across gaping boundaries of faith and heartbreaking circumstances. But we also found ourselves with a much deeper understanding of the desperation that so easily incubates under such circumstances—desperation driven by the desire of the human spirit for justice and a life safe from the constant onslaught of hopelessness and fear.

On top of widespread poverty, many Muslims live in strife- and crisis-ridden regions of the world, and today some 70 percent of the world's refugees are Muslim. The circumstances of war and poverty are difficult for those of us raised in the security and comfort of Western nations to fully grasp. If you happen to be caught in the cycle of poverty, it robs you of dignity and erodes your self-image and self-respect. These issues not only exacerbate the world's cultural and ideological divides, they breed desperate and radical acts. For many in the Muslim world, it is gnawing, relentless hopelessness, not simply ideology, that drives them into the arms of the radical fringe.

———◆———

About a week after the initial invasion of Afghanistan by the United States, things began to noticeably settle down again. We still operated under tight security measures but increasingly felt that much of it was encumbering and unnecessary. Our Mauritanian friends assured us that the disturbance was typical in times of political upheaval but that the dissident voices had largely had their say and would quickly return to their normal lives. For more than a month we had lived rather restricted lives, and many of us, both expatriate and Mauritanian, were ready to resume our more normal routines.

One of the blessings we had during this time, when our movement outside of the home was so restricted, was our house-helper, Aboubacar—a Muslim man from Guinea, a kind and gentle soul who had assisted us for several years with housekeeping and cooking. He was faithfully with us each day, bringing food from the market, preparing wonderful meals, and offering bits of local news that helped us keep tabs on the political and social climate in town. Aboubacar was from the Fula (or Peul) ethnic group—a Muslim people steeped in their faith, with a long tradition of pastoralism in West Africa, herding cattle, goats, and sheep. Shortly after he came to work for us, we learned he cared deeply for his wife and young children. He was sensitive and tenderhearted, and he soon developed a clear affection for each of us, but especially Hannah. We also learned that he eschewed anything that smacked of violence or strife. He would often get quietly distressed when anyone in the house raised his or her voice in a dispute, or even when the discipline of our children resulted in tears (of children or parents).

In a country where it was not particularly common for people to have a soft spot for animals, his tenderness was also extended to the plethora of pets that made their way through our home: dog, cat, rabbit, monkey, and seven hedgehogs. He did not particularly like monkeys in general (he called them a devious and rascally lot), but because he knew of our children's affections for the mischievous monkey that romped around our yard, he eventually developed an affection for the animal, much to our surprise. One day while he was dusting the living room, he stopped me as I passed through and inquired, "Monsieur, may I ask you a rather personal question?"

Somewhat surprised, I replied, "Why certainly, Aboubacar. What is it?"

He turned and hesitantly picked up a framed picture that had always held a prominent place on the cabinet—a picture of Jesus tenderly holding a lamb, part of his face affectionately buried in its fleece. "Since I have been in your house, I have noticed this picture every time I clean the front room. Who is this man?"

I thought about the question carefully for a moment and gently asked, "What is it about him that intrigues you?"

"Well, Monsieur, I was wondering why you have a picture of a man who is obviously so kind to his sheep. Do you mind telling me who this man is and why he has these wounds on his hands?"

I took a deep breath and explained that this was an artist's depiction of *Isa al-Masih* (Jesus the Messiah), the incarnation of a loving God, that he referred to himself as the Good Shepherd who lays down his life for his sheep, and that since my family and I were followers of Jesus, we placed this picture in our home to remind us that he is a kind and gentle shepherd to those who follow him. As I made this explanation Aboubacar was staring intently at the picture, and I saw his eyes twinkle with understanding and evident admiration for a fellow shepherd.

He quietly thanked me, saying, "Now I understand."

Followers of Islam know "about God," and they know of his will as revealed through Mohammed and the precepts of Islam. But God (or Allah) in his essence does not come down among men. In Christ, God has come down to redeem and restore us, and through the incarnation we have the supreme joy and privilege of knowing God in his essence. I hoped that in some small way my words had conveyed such to Aboubacar. In the months that followed, as I passed by the living room when Aboubacar was cleaning, I would often see him gently lift that picture and thoughtfully gaze at it for a few moments before carefully replacing it. And in our conversations that followed, he was clearly pleased to know that the Jesus we followed was gentle and kind.

———•———

Hélène had been pursuing a diploma in music theory by correspondence with the Open University in the United Kingdom—one of the many ways she kept her mind active in this remote outpost. On October 14 she had to fly to Paris to sit for an exam, leaving Hannah and me alone. After the exam she was going to go to her parents' home in Calais, France, to spend a few days before returning. She made all the practical arrangements with Aboubacar for our comfort and nourishment during her planned absence. He fixed Hélène a delicious meal before wishing Madame, as he called her, a safe journey and a quick return. And he assured her he would take good care of Monsieur and *la petite*, as he affectionately referred to Hannah. We then headed out to Nouakchott's small airport on the edge of town, and it was about 9:00 in the evening when Hélène checked in for her 11:00 P.M. flight.

Since we had an hour or more to wait, we sat in the small departure area and chatted. I remember well how nice it was to have this time alone together, temporarily removed from the concerns of family or work. We soon found ourselves reflecting over the past hectic weeks since the twin towers of the World Trade Center had fallen and so many lives had been tragically lost some six thousand miles away.

We also anticipated the future, but this is where we differed. I believed there was every indication that things would continue to return to normal—and every practical signal we had, from local government sources to security references abroad, indicated this. But Hélène is more intuitive about things. She listened, then turned to me and simply said, "Ray, I just don't have a good feeling about leaving you and Hannah here." I gently scoffed at her feelings and suggested she was simply uptight about the flight. (She has spent most of her life flying but has never liked it!) She persisted and repeated her foreboding all the more emphatically. I did not want us to say good-bye on such a negative note, so I begged her to allow herself to have a much-deserved break from the desert, think about herself, and not worry about us. "What's more, we have Aboubacar to take care of us!" I could see that she was still struggling to take my lighthearted and typically male words to heart, especially when she felt so deeply about what she sensed. Loving wife that she is, she snuck a kiss on my cheek in a place that discourages such public acts of affection, gave me a quick, tight hug around the waist, and walked across the tarmac to the waiting plane.

As the plane lifted off into the night sky, I felt grateful that she could have a break from the stressful times and from the loneliness she often felt in Mauritania. But as the last blinking light of the plane merged with the glimmering stars on that clear, desert night, I was already feeling the pangs of being left alone in the desert.

——— 3 ———

A TENUOUS CALM

Do not be afraid. . . . For I will pour water on the
thirsty land, and streams on the dry ground.
(Isaiah 44:2–3)

WEDNESDAY, OCTOBER 17, DAWNED BRIGHT AND RELATIVELY dust-free. It was going to be one of those nice, clear autumn days in the western Sahara when the temperature is relatively mild, never climbing beyond the high nineties. I was looking forward to this day. After a morning of work at the office, I was scheduled to spend the afternoon visiting some of our project sites in the squatter communities that surround the town. I viewed office work as a somewhat tedious but necessary part of my responsibilities: negotiating our many collaborative initiatives by phone or electronic correspondence with our World Vision support offices in the United States, Canada, Europe, and Australia; reviewing budgets and internal audit reports; preparing formal correspondence with government and other partner entities; crafting grant proposals; studying field reports; and seeing to personnel matters—just to name a few of the seemingly endless tasks that usually awaited me each morning in the office.

It was always a relief to get out of the office and away from the administrative tedium to spend time in community neighborhoods, listening to people's stories of concern and hope and learning to better see the world through their eyes. In spite of a heavy administrative load, I tried to carve out regular time for these visits. It was a needed reminder of why we were in Mauritania, sobering on one hand when confronted with the conditions and needs but always uplifting to encounter the vision and enthusiasm of our field staff and the community leaders we worked alongside.

As a result of the difficult times we had endured in recent weeks and the precautionary measures we were under, opportunities to spend time with our communities had been limited. But tensions seemed to be lifting, life was slowly returning to normal, and I was anxious to get back to more regular visits beyond the security and comfort of our office compound.

I shuffled to the kitchen to brew a cup of coffee, a little lonely since Hélène was not there to share our morning ritual. I thought how blessed my family was in spite of all the challenges we had faced recently. Hélène was pursuing her love of art and music; Nathaniel was in a good school in Dakar, Senegal, making friends and quickly growing out of boyhood; and Hannah was crazy about her little school in Nouakchott, which was nestled next door to the American embassy complex.

Besides, I always enjoyed having a few days alone with one of the children. Multitasking has never been one of my favorite duties we are called to in this life, and I was thoroughly enjoying having a few days to focus all my attention while at home on Hannah. On the surface Hannah was a quiet, somewhat shy ten-year-old. She was also active, healthy, and sported an unusually dark tan from her days frolicking on the endless Saharan beaches just outside of town. Hannah was nobody's fool. She was perceptive and had an unusual ability to see through most people. She also carried a spark in her eyes, had a mind of her own, and could be as hardheaded as her father. We were a good match and enjoyed lively discussions over dinner about bugs, dolls, when homework was going to get done, or how we were going to divvy up housecleaning chores until Mom came home.

With these things tumbling around in my mind and knowing that I would not be spending the entire day behind the desk, I was in a particularly upbeat mood as I finished my morning coffee and a time of Scripture reading and reflection. I moved on to Hannah's room to pull open the curtains and coax her into a new day with a light tickle. This was one of those wonderful seasons in her life when she was in love with school. After she was out of bed, there was no lack of motivation to get ready for another fun day. We had our breakfast together, offered a prayer for Mom and Nathaniel, and chatted briefly about our plans for the day ahead. As soon as we had dressed and collected her knapsack and my briefcase, we were out the door.

As I turned off the main thoroughfare onto the side street that led to Hannah's school, we passed a military tank and the armed guards stationed in front of the school and the adjacent American embassy, security precautions offered by the Mauritanian government since the events of 9/11 some five weeks earlier. The instant I pulled the Land Cruiser to a stop in front of the school's shady, gated entrance, Hannah was already leaning over to offer me her usual parting kiss and was bounding out the door before I could wish her a good day. I watched her with an admiring heart as she skipped through the gate in her navy-and-white school uniform with the requisite water jug and knapsack clumsily dangling from her shoulders. After she was safely inside the gate, I drove toward my office, which was only five blocks away. When I passed through our ground floor entrance, I went through my usual ritual of hastily tossing to our receptionist and any other waiting guests greetings of *"As-salaam alaikoum!"* (Peace be upon you) and *"Bonjour!"* before I turned to spring up the stairs of our old building to my second-floor office. Since the steps were uneven and all of them too short, I always took them two or three at a time. This daily exercise baffled our Mauritanian staff who are conditioned by a heritage rich in expectations of propriety and decorum for any type of leader. In my usual haste I would, on occasion, miss a step and stumble briefly while those below tried to stifle chuckles about their American boss who was always in a hurry. I have little doubt they placed bets each day on whether I would make a fool of myself during my entry, but this day I took the entire staircase (two at a time) in stride. When I reached the top I mentally patted myself on the back, thinking it was a good start to what would surely be a good day.

On most occasions, however, I was usually more prudent about meeting expectations when engaging across cultures, especially when I was among local communities that may have had limited exposure to westerners. In our "apprentice" years before coming to Mauritania, Hélène and I had strived to adapt to local culture, learn the language, and basically understand the people we served. This also involved helping them understand us and the cultural baggage and eccentricities we brought along. Sincere as we were, we made many blunders—some funny, others less so.

In my first months in Niger, my research schedule did not allow me the luxury of a formal course in the local Hausa dialect, so I eagerly picked up bits and pieces whenever I could. My enthusiasm, however, prompted premature attempts at practice. Late one afternoon I found myself lost in a remote area, having taken a wrong turn off the dirt track I was following to get to a small village where I hoped to spend the night. In the villages where I worked, I had tried hard to set a wholesome example and to avoid the more common image of male foreigners as whiskey-swilling womanizers.

I was at least thirty minutes from my intended destination, and just as the sun was setting across the low-lying hills, I spotted a group of women returning from their fields, each with a heavy load of firewood on her head. They were obviously startled to see an anxious white man in a motorized vehicle pull up beside them, but I jumped right in with my limited vocabulary and proceeded to ask which path I needed to take to the village where I was headed. Their apprehension turned first to shock, then to unbridled mirth as I struggled with my words, and within a few seconds they all had dropped their loads of wood and fallen to the ground in hysterics. Chatting animatedly among themselves, one of them eventually pointed me in the direction I needed to go. Later that evening, sitting securely around a small fire with village friends and grateful that I was not passing the night lost in the desert bush country, I recounted my experience with the women. When asked to repeat what I had said to them, my friends were instantly seized by the same fits of laughter I had observed earlier. After gathering their wits about them, they patiently explained to me that

I had not asked for the path to their village but for the path to the local brothel.

Some years later, and not long after we had moved to the Sultanate of Oman, Hélène trumped my language blunder in Niger by both our reckonings. In an effort to honor expectations of modesty in the local culture, she always wore a head covering whenever she went out. But being the artist and visually oriented person that she is, she bypassed the standard black scarves and used instead an intricately woven, multicolored piece of cloth she had picked up in the local market. Arabs are nearly always appreciative of Western women who dress modestly and cover their heads, but the odd looks she got over the next month or two with her chosen head covering quickly led me to believe that something was amiss. I begged her to don the more standard black or white scarf, but she would hear nothing of it, stating that she had no intention of sacrificing her artistic tastes in her pursuit of cultural propriety. One day as we were walking into a local restaurant where clients were seated on the carpeted floor, a robed man suddenly jumped to his feet, bowed politely, and in halting English said, "Madame, thank you for trying." After pondering this and other confusing comments that obviously involved her head covering, Hélène finally decided to retire the headpiece and settled for a white scarf, much to my relief. Some weeks later, when I was preparing to travel up-country to visit Rashid, a date-palm grower in the mountains, Hélène handed me the infamous headpiece and suggested I offer it as a gift to Rashid's wife. En route, I handed the colored cloth to my assistant, stating my wife's request. Thinking he had misunderstood me, he said, "You mean you want me to present this to Rashid as a gift, not to his wife." When I asked him why we should do that, he turned and said, "Dr. Norman, this would make a fine gift for Rashid! It is an expensive and high-quality loincloth, traditional underwear for Omani men!"

These were but a few of the many practical blunders we made as we tried to reach across the cultural divides we encountered—embarrassing lessons but profound learning experiences.

———◆———

After my successful (yet culturally risky) assault of the office staircase, I stepped into the office, and my administrative assistant greeted me with her usual warm and reassuring smile. Amrita was a gentle and discerning woman from the beautiful island nation of Sri Lanka off the southern coast of India. An unsung hero, she had traversed her own long, twisting, and difficult journey to find herself now serving God in this remote place. She was a seasoned assistant who had served under a number of national directors, and although she probably did not fully comprehend it, her deep, quiet faith was a welcomed source of inspiration and strength to all of us. Whenever there was a crisis at hand and we were all running around frantically trying to put out the fires, we knew that Amrita was faithfully making the time in the midst of her own busy schedule to take these matters to the throne of grace.

It was about mid-morning when Amrita knocked on my door to tell me she had just received word from both the American and French embassies advising that security measures could be relaxed somewhat, although some minimal measures of caution should still be exercised when outside of the home or office. This confirmed what we had been sensing recently and was welcome news, as we had been operating and living under rather strict protocols for five weeks. My first thoughts were that I could now begin to schedule long-overdue visits to some of our field sites up-country. I mentioned these thoughts to Amrita, who proffered that, while it was good news, I should still exercise caution and prudence when out in public venues, especially in my role as the foreign director of the largest nongovernmental organization (NGO) operating in the country, and a Christian one at that. She had lived here many years and knew the pulse of this country much better than I did; and she offered this advice knowing I would be out that very afternoon visiting nearby project sites.

Life in this corner of the desert is restricted enough during normal times by environmental, cultural, and sociopolitical parameters and expectations, and we were all anxious to get back to the more normal rhythms of life. After Amrita left the room, I found myself thinking about resuming our family's visits to the nearby beaches—one of the few places in the country where we could find much-needed outdoor refreshment and exercise. For many, both expatriate and Mauritanian, the long stretches of wild, open, and usually empty beaches were a wonderful respite from the rigors of Nouakchott life and the oppressive heat. On weekends my family and I frequently joined other staff members for an afternoon of relaxation and fun. In normal times we made short trips to the beach nearly every week for a walk, a swim, or some type of water sport. These trips offered a complete break from the routine and always helped us feel we had restored some level of sanity to our crazy lives. Over the years we had developed a plethora of beach activities to pass the time: surfing, kayaking, or skiing in the surf with the assistance of a double-length ski rope attached to a four-wheel-drive vehicle driven along the open beach. Each one in our family, including Hannah, is a strong, experienced swimmer, and we knew how to handle ourselves in the often-turbulent surf and unpredictable currents.

After 9/11, however, we had adopted a policy that expatriate staff members should not spend time on the beach unless in the company of others and with at least two vehicles. Although some in the expatriate community continued to visit the beach, most of us at World Vision refrained—a precautionary measure until we were sure things had indeed returned to normal.

I picked up the phone and called Brock, an American friend whose daughter, Hilary, was Hannah's best friend. I told him of the announcement from the two embassies and asked if he and Hilary would be interested in joining Hannah and me for a late-afternoon swim and perhaps some surfing. Brock was interested but not sure if he would be able to get away in time, so he agreed to let me know beforehand if he was going to make it. I made a few calls to other friends and told them that some of us were likely to make a beach run later that day.

I finished most of the important tasks on my desk shortly after midday, and after a quick lunch I left the office with my driver for our field offices in the outlying squatter communities of El Mina and Sebkha. Once there we were joined by field staff, who briefed me on recent progress as we drove out into the community to visit a newly constructed maternity clinic and some recently installed water delivery outlets.

Access to health facilities and clean water was largely unheard of in these communities prior to World Vision's assistance. Community members had contributed to these efforts with both their financial resources and labor, and it was always heartwarming to see their excitement and delight as these efforts came to fruition. I was also keenly aware that the transformation of poor communities into communities of hope, which I was privileged to witness firsthand, was only possible because of the many people in the United States and elsewhere around the world who took seriously the commands of Jesus to love their neighbor and to love the poor.

What I saw with my own eyes was not a glowing, full-color report in a brochure or a well-scripted television clip about the benefits of Christian humanitarian work. Rather, this was the real thing in all its raw integrity. The communities were still dirty; people still suffered in ways impossible to describe adequately. But what I witnessed on these visits were tangible signs of progress, hope, and confirmation that a difference truly was being made in the lives of the poor for the sake of Christ. And I was grateful that, in the midst of the restrictions we had to work under, we had consistently been open about our identity and our motivations— that we were a Christian organization that in obedience to Christ's command sought simply to help the poor; that our practice of partnering with communities reflected how we as Christians chose to live out our own faith; and that our love for them was our response to being loved by Christ.

To our Muslim friends, loving and caring was not considered proselytizing, nor was offense taken when we were open about the reason and source of our love. Many Muslims regard Jesus as the prophet of love, and they readily expect true followers of Jesus to be people of love. But they rarely see this in the few foreigners they encounter who call themselves Christian.

Of course, for the Christian, Jesus is far more than just a prophet or proclaimer of love. He is the actual source of our love, the author of love itself. And to the extent we could, we faithfully tried to let that love flow freely in all our words and deeds as we labored alongside Mauritania's poor. Our expressions of love and care in the name of Christ were, for the most part, readily accepted.

The new maternity clinic in the El Mina squatter community stood in stark contrast to the surrounding squalor—a beacon of hope reflected in the faces and conversations of the women of the community who toured the modest facility with me, as well as a silent, shining reflection of the love of countless caring and generous Christians from around the world. Most Mauritanian women do not have even remote access to such a facility. For most expectant mothers childbirth takes place on a floor mat in the family's mud house or tent, with little or no recourse if things go badly. And if both mother and child survive the birthing process, poor, unhygienic, postnatal care often takes a high toll.

I inspected the delivery room and the postnatal-care wing of this small facility, then spent some time chatting with the others from the community and the local mayor's office who had joined us. This clinic was also the fruit of a collaborative effort among World Vision, municipal administrators, and the community, and I was particularly delighted that we all could take pride in the fruit of our efforts in having made this important facility a reality in the community.

The last site we visited that day was a potable water-holding tank in Sebkha, one outlet of a much larger, community-wide water delivery network. Individuals or secondary water vendors obtained water from outlets for a small fee that was invested in a fund managed by the community and used for the system's maintenance and upkeep. I examined the quality of the construction and chatted with community members about their views on clean water and its fundamental role in reducing the incidence of common debilitating diseases, especially those that threatened their young children.

As a water engineer by training, I could not help but ponder the similarities between this network that facilitated the flow of clean, safe water and our own roles as vessels through which Christ's love could readily flow to those I stood with under the warm afternoon sun. This was not idealistic or presumptuous spiritual reflection. The challenges and discrepancies in my analogy were uncomfortably evident. I was keenly aware that our recently installed water network might provide more reliable delivery of a life-giving substance than would the earthen vessel I inhabited. Sustainable delivery of clean water in the desert can be accomplished with good science and careful planning, a task that seemed less daunting than the task of effectively and faithfully positioning oneself as a vessel for the flow of Christ's love. For most water projects in this part of the world, the installation of the system (be it pumps, pipes, or holding tanks) is the easy part. Their upkeep and maintenance over the long term is the more challenging undertaking. And so it is with the heart. Being stirred or inspired to help the poor in the name of Christ is only the first step, and usually the easiest. Keeping one's heart clear of prejudice, self-interest, pessimism, and other clogging influences is a more complex undertaking, and it requires commitment to daily, faithful maintenance.

As I moved toward the waiting vehicle to leave, I offered a silent, desperate petition to God. Not only did I pray that this small project would be seen as a reflection of his care and love, but I found myself beseeching him to—in some way, in any way—mold me and my colleagues into more willing and pliable vessels for his use, for the ready flow of his love to the people of this dry and thirsty land.

---— 4 —---

PETALS OF BLOOD

My prayer is not that you take them out of the world
but that you protect them from the evil one.
(JOHN 17:15)

UNDER OUR PRESENT SECURITY MEASURES, A DRIVER FROM THE
office took staff children to their homes from the school in the
early afternoon. In Hélène's absence, Aboubacar was there to
welcome Hannah home, give her a snack, and watch over her
until I returned from work later in the afternoon. Hannah loved
Aboubacar and trusted him implicitly, as did the rest of us. During
Hélène's short absence, Aboubacar would prepare a stack of fresh
pancakes, which he knew were Hannah's favorite, instead of the
usual and more modest milk and cookie as an after-school treat.
I only learned this much later. It was their little secret, but it
explained why Hannah often did not have much of an appetite at
dinner on those days when I played Mr. Mom.

As I drove back into town around 4:30 P.M., I gave Hannah a call at the house with my cell phone, explained to her in simple terms what I had learned earlier about the relaxation of security measures, and asked if she wanted to make a short visit to the beach before dinner. Though she was already deeply engaged with her Barbie dolls, she agreed to go—perhaps more because of my excitement than her own. The prospect that her friend Hilary might join us there was an added incentive.

When I drove up to the house a little before 5:00 P.M., Hannah was wearing a lime-green summer dress covered with cherries and orange-slice patterns over a purple bathing suit with a butterfly print—a gift recently mailed to her by her grandmother. I grabbed a towel and a pair of shorts, along with a few other items for the beach, and in a few minutes we were bouncing over one of the small tracks that wound through the low-lying sand dunes north of town.

I still did not have firm confirmation from Brock or the others I had called earlier in the day, but if they could not join us, it was very possible we would find others we knew enjoying the beach on this fine afternoon. I told Hannah we would drive out to our usual beach spot and join up with whomever we found there. If no one was at the beach, it would have been worth the try and we would just head back home and go again another day.

As we drove, Hannah and I chatted about her day at school, her friends, and Mom's anticipated return home in another week or so. The isolated track we followed paralleled the beach about a quarter of a mile inland. Fifteen minutes north of town, after weaving between small dunes and dodging the odd, grazing camel, I turned west toward the beach and stopped the vehicle at the base of a large range of dunes that separate the salt flats from the beach itself. These dunes rise to a height of fifty feet or more, and after I engaged the four-wheel drive and deflated the tires, it would only take two to three minutes to cross the dunes and arrive on the hard-packed beach. Deflating tires enhances the vehicle's traction in soft sand and is a ritual we regularly went through when traveling to the beach or to remote sites up-country.

It was still rather warm, and the ocean breeze was blowing up sand from the dunes. As I stepped out of the vehicle I left it idling, with the air conditioner running and the windows up. I stretched briefly and took in the quiet surroundings—an endless horizon of sand dunes with the gentle sound of the hidden surf a short distance away.

One of the things I loved most about my line of work was that it took me to some of the most remote places that people inhabit on this globe. For many the desert is only a harsh and threatening environment, but in my years in the Sahara and in Arabia I had learned not only how to survive and live unthreatened by its sharp edges, but also to cherish the isolation and stark beauty it offered. It was the first time in five weeks I had been out of Nouakchott's teeming confines, and I savored the quiet, isolated moment. Years before, I had been asked by someone what I loved most about Africa, aside from its people. Before I had really tried to process the question, I surprised myself by blurting out, "The great silences. What I love most about Africa are its great silences."

Wherever you travel in Africa, outside of its growing urban centers, you can always encounter the cleansing wonder of natural silence that accosts your senses like a flood of fresh water in a parched landscape. That day near the beach, the soft silence was only interrupted by the swirl of sand off the dunes or the occasional drop of the distant surf, and after savoring it for a few moments I took a small tool from my pocket and knelt down by the front driver-side wheel to turn the four-wheel-drive hub lock and begin releasing air from the tires.

After a few moments I heard a movement and glanced over my shoulder to see a light-skinned Arab man emerge from the dunes and approach the vehicle. He was carrying a small plastic bag and was dressed in typical Mauritanian garb—a flowing blue robe with his head wrapped in a full-cover turban, leaving only his eyes exposed to the elements. There was nothing alarming about his presence, since the beach corridor served as the primary route for occasional north-south travel for both pedestrians and the occasional four-wheel-drive vehicle. There was little chance of losing one's way, and at low tide it provided a firm and easily walkable pathway through what was otherwise loose and shifting desert sand. I presumed he was approaching me to request a lift into town—again, a fairly common request when encountering lone pedestrians on this stretch of the beach. When he got within about ten feet, I heard his *"As-salaam alaikoum"* greeting, and I stood to my feet and returned the Arabic greeting. As I did so, I glanced at Hannah in the front passenger seat and noticed she paid little interest to the passing stranger and was obviously preoccupied with her daydreaming or self-examination in the side-view mirror, as young girls will do.

As is the case in many parts of the Muslim world, an extended greeting and formal exchange of queries about one's health, family, and livestock is requisite etiquette before engaging in any conversation. The formality is expected of every member of Mauritanian society, whether rich, poor, noble, or of slave origin; and unlike the cursory greetings in many Western cultures, the formal exchange implicitly conveys the message that each person is of value and has an important role to fulfill in society. So even in my haste to get to the beach, I took the time to greet this lone stranger.

Before the formal exchange was over, we had switched to French, and the man's command of the language indicated he was probably well-educated. In a clear and polite voice, he asked where we were headed, and I responded we were going away from town toward the beach to meet friends for a short walk or swim. He then casually glanced at the World Vision logo on the vehicle, inquired briefly about my line of work, and asked if I was an American.

Given the circumstances I probably should have been alarmed by the question about my nationality, but I had been asked such questions before and thought nothing of it. Most Western expatriates were French and generally less known for their casual friendliness than the few Americans working in the country. So I judged his query to simply be a response to the polite and friendly manner with which I had engaged him. He seemed to want to linger but soon said good-bye and headed toward town.

I bent down again by the front tire, but after a few seconds he addressed me again. "Monsieur!" Thinking he had another question for me, I stood and faced him. To my complete shock I found he was about three paces away—with a large, nine-millimeter pistol aimed at my chest.

In an instant all the pieces flew together in my mind: the heightened security, his query about my nationality, the way in which he lingered and had obviously tried to draw out the conversation, and even the fact that a relatively well-educated person was afoot on this lonely track. I hoped against hope that all he wanted was to rob me of cash or even the vehicle. I immediately tried to engage him in conversation again, attempting to ascertain exactly what he wanted. But after he hesitated only a few seconds and made no reply to my queries, I saw the muscles in his hands tense as he deliberately began to squeeze the trigger. His intention was crystal clear.

I reacted instantaneously, first ducking, then lunging for the nearby door, throwing it open and hurling myself into the driver's seat. I was hoping to find a split second in which I could shift the idling vehicle into first gear and accelerate out of harm's way before the first shot could be fired. It was foolish thinking, of course, but it was the only alternative I saw that offered even a glimmer of hope in that instant.

We had been standing just behind Hannah's field of vision, so she was entirely unaware of what had transpired in these past few moments. As I jumped into the front seat and locked the door, I shouted to my shocked daughter, "Hannah! Get down! Get down!" But being jolted out of her peaceful reverie, Hannah's natural reaction was to first figure out what all the commotion was about. As I desperately tried to shove her out of the seat to the floor, she glanced over my shoulder toward my window, and I saw her eyes fill with shock and fear.

"Dad! That man has a gun!" she screamed. I swung around to see that he was already at the window aiming the gun at my head. In that fraction of a second, I knew with certainty that I would not be able to put the vehicle in gear and speed away before he could fire. Trying to get Hannah down had cost me precious milliseconds.

From the moment the assailant's intention first became clear, I knew the chances that I would survive this were essentially non-existent. All of my crashing thoughts coalesced toward one single goal: saving my daughter's life. As I tried to stay focused on this objective, I desperately fought back the barrage of intruding questions that screamed at me: *Why? How? What if . . . ?* Those questions greedily tried to eat away the precious seconds I might have left. In my mind and heart I was already gone, but I was going to try everything I could in those last moments to give Hannah even the slimmest chance of survival.

In the next instant the man fired three shots at my temple in rapid succession—click, click, click—and each time the gun misfired. This extraordinary but fleeting interlude did not produce even the slightest notion in my mind that my chances were bettered, only that I still had (wonder of wonders) another second or two to extend Hannah's chances. The assailant was obviously frustrated. In one quick movement he tapped the malfunctioning gun with his free hand and then, to my complete horror, he took aim directly at Hannah—probably because of her screams. Something innate rose up within me. I have no doubt my action had at its source the love that only God can put in a father's heart for his daughter. Every created, human fiber within me rose up in that instant. Shouting, "No! No! No!" I threw my chest and arms up against the window in the hope of blocking the oncoming shots. Perhaps once the man saw that I was gone, he would spare Hannah.

In that instant, my world and Hannah's exploded. The next few seconds were the longest in my life. Even today, as I struggle with the memory of that moment, it comes back to me in frame-by-frame clicks of my mind's projector: the deafening report of the gun instantly ushering in an eerie and silent world broken only by the distant ringing in my ears, the simultaneous burst of flying glass, the silent explosion of blood and sinew from my right arm, followed by a scream and the dull thump of Hannah's body against the far passenger door. Milliseconds seemed to turn into minutes, and out of that numb, ringing fog in my head, I slowly realized I was still alive, and God had given me yet another fleeting instant to try to save Hannah, who was groaning from the shock of it all in the seat beside me. I saw the assailant quickly taking aim again, but since much of the fractured glass still remained in the window it was obvious he was finding it difficult to get either of us in his sights. During his brief hesitation I slammed the vehicle into gear and shoved the accelerator to the floor. As I did, the shots aimed at my head hit my headrest and the metal window frame only inches away as we spun off. I ducked my head, and his remaining few shots took out our rear window as I distanced us from where he was standing.

Within a few seconds there was only the low hum of our four wheels in the sand of the low-lying dunes and the occasional thump when we hit a patch of firm ground or a small bush as we sped away. I thought it likely the assailant was accompanied by others who had a vehicle hidden close by among the dunes and would soon give pursuit. I had been driving as fast as I could with my head down, glancing occasionally just over the edge of the front dashboard to find my way. After we were out of gunshot range, I carefully raised my head to see if anyone was following us. To my surprise and relief there was no one in sight, even at the place of assault some two hundred yards back. I still did not want to take any chances, so I maintained a significant speed, winding furiously over and around sand dunes with the intention of circling widely back southward toward the relative safety of town. I was unsure as to whether this was a lone attack or part of a larger coordinated effort back in town, so I decided I would try to approach town cautiously if I could get that far.

Within two or three minutes, I began to assess the situation within the vehicle. I knew I had sustained a serious wound in my right arm and for the first time glanced down and saw a gaping hole a few inches below my shoulder where the bullet had exited. Strands of muscle tissue hung from its jagged edges, looking strangely like the petals of a withered flower. Rallying my thoughts, I realized I had somehow managed to shift gears with my right arm, so I presumed that there were no shattered bones. But I was losing blood. My shirt and shorts were already soaked, so I quickly whispered a prayer that I would stay conscious long enough to get Hannah to safety. I had a cell phone, but I knew we were well beyond the town's limited coverage area. Using up precious time to place a call for help would be fruitless.

Assessing myself only took a couple of seconds, but I was more concerned about Hannah, as I knew she must be terrified and that she likely had small glass splinters in her eyes from the powerful spray of the shattering window. I had heard an occasional whimper from her over the past few minutes, and in the periphery of my forward-focused vision, I could tell she was lying, curled up tightly, on the seat next to me. As soon as I reached a relatively obstacle-free stretch of sand, I turned to glance at her. Hannah was grasping the front of her dress. I was shocked to see that she was lying in a small pool of blood that had gathered in the seat. Glancing hurriedly back and forth between Hannah and the route ahead of me, I reached over and took the hand that was clutching the front of her dress and gingerly pulled it back. Underneath her hand I saw that the front of her dress and her bathing suit were soaked in blood. Her eyes were closed. I gently pulled the front of her bathing suit down to get a clear look at her small, heaving chest, thinking she had perhaps been cut by a flying shard of glass. What I saw was the last thing I expected, and it shook me to the core of my soul. In the center of her chest, some four inches below her neckline, was a deep, clean bullet hole, out of which blood was softly flowing.

My world had already crumbled, but this was when it imploded with a force I had never before experienced. At that moment the very bottom of my life seemed to drop out, leaving in an instant a sucking void, a black chasm into which disbelief and raw fear came mercilessly crashing in.

I felt a cry come welling up from the depths of my soul, but when it reached my mouth, there was no sound; only a feeble, suffocating gasp came out that did no justice to the intensity of raw emotion within me. The loud protest I craved to utter just wouldn't come. But the feeble gasps that did come, I know now, were aimed at God. "No, Lord! This is *not* how it was supposed to be! Just moments ago my life was to be forfeited, not hers. I surrendered *my* life to you at the beginning of this journey. It was I who counted the cost, took up my cross, and offered *my* life to serve this nation and its people. Not Hannah! Don't take my daughter for the sake of the call you placed on my life."

At the birth of each of our children, I had consecrated them to God the instant they were placed in my arms. I had asked that he mold and use their lives for his purposes, that they too would hunger after and pursue him and discover for themselves the joy and fulfillment in life that is found only in serving him. Even before her birth, I had a deep sense that God had a special purpose for Hannah's life—that he was going to shape and use her in a special way. But what I was witnessing at that moment flew in the face of my deep certainty. As these thoughts raced through my mind, I saw Hannah open her eyes and reach for the front of her bloody dress to see for herself what I had seen. I begged her not to look, but it was too late and her curiosity too high. She examined the hole in her chest and then asked with tempered incredulity, "Daddy, have I been shot?"

"Yes, Hannah, you have been shot."

She thought for a moment and then with the same soft and measured voice asked, "Am I going to die now?"

Her question, saturated with an innocence that can only come from a child, almost tore my heart apart. She and I had a father-daughter routine when I wanted her to pay careful attention to my words: I would place my middle and index fingers under my eyes and ask Hannah to meet my gaze as I spoke. So raising my right arm, I pointed to my eyes with my fingers. "Hannah, look up and listen to me carefully." I did this spontaneously, knowing I had to say something but not really knowing what it should be. As she raised her eyes to mine, I found myself saying with firm conviction, "You are not going to die. You are going to live."

My own words surprised me. They were words of affirmation and faith that came from somewhere deep within. Although they were meant for Hannah, they brought with them the relief and comfort my emotions had sought through my failed attempt to shout down fear and reality a moment earlier. But it was at that moment, as Hannah was looking up at me, that she first noticed my own blood-soaked shirt and wounded arm.

"Daddy!" she cried out in alarm. "Have *you* been shot?"

"Yes, Hannah, I have been shot as well."

"Are you about to die?"

The prospect that I could die seemed to shake Hannah far more deeply than the possibility of her own death. "Look at me again, Hannah," I said, again pointing at my eyes in an attempt to get her gaze off of my bloodied arm. "I am not about to die either," I said firmly as I locked my eyes with hers. "We just need to get to safety and help as quickly as we can." I desperately wanted to keep her alert and cognizant, because I knew if she began to fade or lost consciousness, I would have to stop the vehicle in this remote and insecure location, and in the process lose valuable time on which her life might depend. "But I need your help, Hannah. You pray, and I'll focus on driving and getting us to safety as quickly as I can."

"Okay, Daddy," she replied softly but firmly. She immediately closed her eyes and began, "Jesus . . . Jesus . . . Jesus . . . please help us get home safely."

All this time I had been flying across the desert landscape at as high a speed as I dared, swerving around the larger dunes and dodging the occasional bush. As I turned to focus on the route I was taking, I again tried to assess our situation and what the chances were of Hannah's survival. In spite of my effort to protect her, the bullet that had gone through my arm had obviously pierced Hannah's chest.

The bullet hole ran deep, and I reasoned that since her heart was still beating, the bullet was likely lodged somewhere adjacent to her heart. But if this were the case, it would have pierced her lung, which would normally result in internal bleeding and possible suffocation from her lung filling with blood. As she continued to call out the name of Jesus with a soft but firm voice, I kept listening for the sound of choking and looking for blood in her mouth. I was surprised that I heard and saw neither.

Part of me was sure Hannah would die within the next few minutes, but another part refused to let go. Every new second that she lived gave me a small measure of hope. At the same time I also took up my plea with God once again. "Don't take my daughter for the sake of the call you placed on my life. She has her own life to live. She must live to one day hear and respond to your call on her life for herself."

As I was silently and frantically pleading my case before God, there were other emotions tumbling around on the inside.

Looking back, I recall no emotion of anger. But I felt shocked and hurt—deeply hurt. The feeling surprised and confused me. It was unexpected, and I was unsure what it meant. My thoughts were racing, scrambling for an answer. *How could one of the people for whom God had given me such a deep and genuine love try to kill me and my daughter with such deliberate and callous intent? Surely if the assailant knew how much we cared about him and his people he would never have done this.* This hurt was not an emotion that stayed with me for a long time. It was short-lived, but intense. And it seemed to come flooding in when I contemplated the possibility that my time of service to this land, to these people, might be coming to an abrupt end. In a moment I rallied my thoughts back to the present: I was still here, still alive, and in spite of the extraordinary circumstances, I still felt as called as ever to love and serve these people. I had to focus on getting Hannah to safety, and not an ounce of energy or even a second of my time could be wasted on unpacking these feelings. It would have to wait until later.

Some ten minutes had transpired since we first encountered the assailant. I was slowly getting the sense, for reasons I could not fully understand, that Hannah was not about to die in the next few minutes. Miraculously, she remained lucid, and there was an obvious strength in her voice as she continued to pray.

A reassuring moment came when, in the middle of her invocations, she stopped and once again examined the bullet's damage to her chest. Without taking her eyes off her wound, she commented straightforwardly, "Daddy, that man put a hole in my new bathing suit!" I was flabbergasted. This was not my wounded daughter who was about to die at any moment. This was the ten-year-old daughter I was accustomed to—already painfully self-conscious about her appearance and absolutely crazy about any new piece of clothing from America or Europe. Stunned by her words, if not her spunk, all I could do was mutter, "Well, yes, Hannah, I see. We'll just have to deal with that later." Apparently satisfied with my response, she laid her head back down in her bloodied seat and continued her supplications to Jesus. But her words had flooded me with relief and a renewed conviction that if I could just get her to help in time, there was still an ever-so-slim chance that she might survive.

We were still a mile or two from the edge of town, and I was also worried about my own blood loss. I was concerned that I could lose consciousness at any moment, possibly resulting in a vehicle accident. More worrying was the possibility of Hannah being left wounded and without help in an isolated location on the outskirts of town. As we neared town I guessed there was a chance we were in range of a cell tower. I grabbed my phone from my shorts pocket, but when I tried to look at the keys and screen they were illegible from my bloodied hand. As I drove I frantically looked for a dry, bloodless spot on my shirt or shorts where I could wipe the phone clean, but I found none.

Eventually I was able to wipe the phone (and my hand) under my relatively bloodless left armpit and dial the World Vision office. It had long since closed, and there was a good chance no one would answer. But World Vision accountants are notorious for working late, and a flood of relief passed over me when I heard the voice of Beverly, our Canadian finance director, on the other end of the line. So as not to alarm her, in the calmest voice I could manage I explained our circumstances and asked her to alert Dr. Sheikh, who had a small clinic just behind our World Vision offices.

Dr. Sheikh was a gracious French national married to a Mauritanian man, and she had set up a small practice in Nouakchott. Many of our staff used her for minor medical issues, as reliable medical facilities and personnel were extremely limited in Mauritania. And this was my primary concern; even if I were able to get Hannah to town before something terrible happened, there were no emergency or surgery facilities such as we know in America or Europe. Any type of surgery to safely remove a bullet lodged deep in Hannah's chest was out of the question in Nouakchott. The nearest facilities and medical personnel who could possibly perform such a procedure were in Dakar, a difficult five-hour drive or forty-five minutes by a plane that only operated a few days of the week.

I recalled that Amrita's home was near this edge of town, so I told Beverly that I would go there first to see if I could find someone to help get us to Dr. Sheikh's office; however, if we did not show up in about fifteen minutes, someone should come looking for us, as I was not sure how much longer I would be able to maintain consciousness.

I swung into the front of Amrita's house a few minutes later and struggled to the door, hoping none of her neighbors would see us and create unnecessary alarm. But to my dismay I found no one there. After banging on the door I stumbled back to the vehicle as quickly as I could in my condition and found that Hannah seemed to be fading. The shock and adrenaline had begun to wear off, and Hannah murmured that she was beginning to feel cold and tired. I urged her to hold on for another ten minutes, and during the remainder of our drive I tried to maintain a running conversation with her, all the while silently tossing petitions heavenward that I too would maintain consciousness.

Within ten minutes I pulled in front of the doctor's small clinic, having negotiated the streets and traffic of Nouakchott at a relatively high speed with an obviously shot-out vehicle. I was relieved to find a small group of waiting individuals, including Beverly, Dr. Sheikh, and a handful of her staff. As I pulled to a stop and those around opened our doors and began attending to us, a flood of relief swept over me; we were no longer facing this crisis alone.

But my relief was only momentary. As the doctor leaned over Hannah in her seat, I silently motioned for her to examine Hannah's chest. At this point Hannah was not very alert, and the instant the doctor saw her wound, she quickly shot me a glance and shook her head firmly—sending the clear but silent message that things did not look good. She obviously did not want Hannah to know her first prognosis, but she clearly did not want me to get my hopes up. For me her message was clear: given the circumstances, Hannah did not stand much of a chance.

Although others were trying to coax me from my seat, I dropped my head to the steering wheel and poured out yet another prayer, but one that was more fervent, more absolute, more final than perhaps any I have ever prayed. In that moment I stormed into heaven's throne room and stated my case in resounding detail, but on the outside my only audible words through my folded arms were a raspy, "Oh, Lord, you can have me if this is the cost you require of me. *But not my daughter.* Not my daughter!" In that moment I felt that everything within me was turned inside out; every part of my inner being was laid bare, exposed, and vulnerable before God as never before or since.

I was so weakened from both the physical trauma and my spiritual battle that I reluctantly gave in to those who were trying to quickly but gently move me to the back seat. In a few moments Moctar, our World Vision director for administrative affairs and human resources, was behind the wheel. Dr. Sheikh was in the rear seat with me, behind Hannah, and under the doctor's directions we were speeding off to another clinic equipped with a functioning X-ray machine. Amazingly, a French pediatrician on a short-term assignment in Nouakchott was going to meet us at our next stop. When we arrived he and Dr. Sheikh whisked Hannah away on a waiting stretcher, and within minutes X-rays were being made of her chest to try to locate the bullet.

As I stepped out of the vehicle, I was surprised at the size of the crowd outside the clinic. Word was already out that a foreigner had been shot, and both the curious and concerned were assembling in the street. I noted a few policemen around and was informed that the marine guards from the American embassy were on their way to work with local authorities to cordon off the area and monitor the crowd for security purposes, since the circumstances of the shooting were still unknown. I later learned that a crowd of about four hundred people had gathered around the small clinic within the hour.

I thought I would follow Hannah, but instead I was taken to another area for medical treatment of my wound. The instant I realized I was not where Hannah was being examined I insisted (somewhat belligerently) that I join her. With a tourniquet tied around my upper arm to staunch the bleeding, and against the clinic staff's protests, I stumbled to the X-ray area, where I found a number of our Mauritanian staff, along with other officials, anxiously waiting in the hallway for news about Hannah's prognosis. They each greeted me warmly and quietly. I then made my way to Hannah's side and squeezed her hand, letting her know I was back with her.

In a few moments the developed X-ray was rushed to the two doctors, who with their assistants began hovering over Hannah and were soon glancing quickly back and forth between her and the X-ray, murmuring. The X-ray showed no bullet in Hannah's chest area, but did indicate one down near her waist where she had no evident wound. While they pondered the X-ray results, a wise medical assistant began feeling around the folds of Hannah's dress near her waistline and found the bullet. As they began cleaning the blood from the rest of her abdomen, they found a small exit hole near Hannah's armpit. In an instant the truth became clear. The bullet had entered the center of her chest and hit her sternum, but having been slowed down by the window glass and my arm, rather than penetrating farther, it had glanced off her sternum, passed along the exterior of her rib cage, and exited near her armpit. The bullet had not penetrated her lungs or her heart; she was seriously hurt, but not in mortal danger! The murmurings of those huddled around Hannah were replaced with sighs of relief, and the pediatrician turned around and told me the amazing news that even he was trying to grasp.

By this time the small room and the hallway outside were packed shoulder to shoulder with our staff, government officials, embassy staff, and others. They grew instantly silent as they listened to the doctor's words directed at an anxious father. In the hot, stifling press of that largely Muslim crowd, I felt the crushing, threatening burden of hopelessness loosen and lift from my shoulders, and I turned my eyes upward and unashamedly uttered my thanks to God. "Thank you, thank you, oh, faithful and loving Father." As I said these words, the healing tears at last began to flow. Joy and relief, as well as tears, were soon expressed around the room and shared equally between Muslim and Christian, American and Arab, black and white, and just about every color in between.

———•———

A short time later Hannah and I were reclining on adjacent beds. We were wrapped in bandages with intravenous drips in our arms. With the fluids making up for her loss of blood, Hannah began to revive. In spite of being in a spartan facility in a remote desert town, for the first time in several hours we both began to relax. Our most troubling discomfort was under our thin, single sheets. Our bloodstained clothes had been removed or cut away, and the area around our wounds had been cleaned. But Hannah had been left with no clothes or even underclothes, and I had only my undershorts, still partially stained with blood. With medical staff, World Vision staff, and other officials constantly moving in and out of the room, I was not about to let my last piece of human dignity go with those undershorts. Hannah had not been so fortunate and told me so in the desperate but fervent whisper of a frightfully embarrassed ten-year-old girl.

But there was little either of us could do. With the intravenous drips in our arms, our bladders were constantly in need of emptying. I would trundle off to the toilet holding my intravenous drip in one hand, pressing the elbow of my wounded arm against a sheet to keep it wrapped tightly against my torso, and solemnly greeting officials who milled about in the hallway as I passed in my undignified state. Hannah was forced to make do with a bedpan while attendants stood around—an exercise she would later claim was "the most difficult experience of the entire day."

Shortly after we were moved to our beds, the American ambassador, Jon, and his wife, Shaparak, arrived. He was a seasoned diplomat who had spent more than four hundred days in captivity during the Iran hostage crisis of 1979–81. Visits by the chief commissioner for Investigation Services and the Mauritanian director for National Security followed. In the midst of the commotion and the constant coming and going of different people at our bedsides, I kept an eye on Hannah; I was concerned she would be completely overwhelmed. But her demeanor surprised me. She met everyone's gaze with a warm, quiet smile and responded kindly and gently to every query. In spite of all she had been through, she was obviously at peace.

The ambassador and his wife were our good friends, and they greeted us warmly. They immediately asked if I had called my wife. When I told them I had not, the ambassador gave me his cell phone, and his wife urged me to call immediately. This was not going to be easy, and they saw my hesitation. I loved Hélène dearly and did not want to distress her, especially since she had a premonition that something was not right only hours before her departure a week earlier. I had dismissed it, but she had left with a genuine concern for our safety, and I now had to tell her that her discernment had been right-on. Under the insistent stares of my two bedside guests, I took a deep breath and dialed France.

Hélène was surprised at my unexpected call, so I quickly explained that Hannah and I were okay, but that there had been an incident near the beach. I then took a deep breath and briefly explained the events, assuring her that Hannah was now in stable condition beside me here in the clinic and was waiting to talk with her.

Hélène stayed remarkably calm, but I could tell there were a hundred questions thundering through her mind. I quickly said, "Listen, Hélène. Shaparak and Jon are standing next to me, so I will pass the phone to them so they can explain the details and answer your questions."

It was one of the more difficult telephone calls I had ever made, and over the next ten minutes, the ambassador and his wife graciously and patiently explained everything to my anxious wife. She was soon chatting with Hannah, much to Hannah's delight, and was surprised at the strength of her daughter's voice. I then signed off with Hélène, explaining that Hannah and I would soon be medically evacuated.

After my call to Hélène, the director of National Security, the chief commissioner, and a couple of their staff asked to have some time with us. Understandably they were keen to know the details of the incident. Both men were polite and asked their questions gently. They were obviously intrigued by Hannah's spunk, given what she had just been through, and the chief commissioner seemed particularly taken by Hannah's peaceful demeanor and her persistent smile. We did our best to describe the details of the incident but were of limited help when asked to describe the assailant—and this was obviously their greatest interest.

At the time Mauritania was a little-known country whose leadership was struggling to come out from under the reputation of being an isolated, backwater place where pockets of Islamic extremism bubbled and burped out of its rocky and sandy expanse. This incident was not what Mauritania needed, especially in the immediate aftermath of 9/11 and the negative international press received since then. Early in our discussion and before I had the opportunity to give them my take on the motive for the incident, one of the men proffered, "It was obviously just a robbery; he clearly wanted your vehicle." I explained that, in my attempt to engage the assailant in conversation when he first pulled the gun on me, I had asked him if he wanted my vehicle. Given his lack of response and his actions that followed, I knew with certainty that this had been no simple robbery attempt. It was obvious these officials were anxious to save face, and diplomatic expediency called for an official account that would soothe concerns and not inflame them.

After the officials left I was surprised to see my friend Brock and his daughter Hilary walk into the room. I was touched that Brock would bring Hilary to see Hannah, given the obvious risk of frightening her and overwhelming her with the tenuous security of the situation, the commotion of police and armed guards around the clinic, and the sight of her best friend lying freshly wounded before her. Their courageous and selfless act spoke deeply to both of us, especially Hannah, who was delighted beyond words to find her best friend at her bedside.

The situation was obviously hard on Hilary, as she spent most of the time crying quietly at Hannah's beside while Hannah tried to console her with smiles and assurances that she would be okay. Hannah has always carried the memory of this special moment.

As it had turned out, Brock and Hilary had not been able to make it to the beach that afternoon. As we chatted, it slowly dawned on Brock and me that had they been there, it could well have been him and his daughter who encountered the assailant.

Following my description of the incident and where it had occurred, the police had their men on the beach taking nearly every suspicious lone traveler in the area into custody. Later that evening the chief commissioner and the director of National Security came back into our room and in lowered voices asked me if Hannah and I would be willing to look at a lineup of individuals they had rounded up in the general vicinity of the assault. I was a little dubious at how this would work, as the assailant had been wearing a traditional robe with his head wrapped in a turban, making it nearly impossible to positively identify the individual even if he had been caught. Hannah had been through enough for one day, and I was worried about the alarm she might feel at the possibility of facing her assailant once again. I quickly expressed my doubts and concern to the two gentlemen and told them I was willing to see the lineup in another room.

But they insisted that we involve Hannah, stressing the point that two memories are better than one and that with each passing hour, the chances of finding the man significantly decreased. So after asking to be left alone with Hannah, I explained the request and told her that, while I would be seeing the lineup, she should not feel under any pressure to do this with me. I should not have been surprised that, even in her condition, Hannah's spunk and curiosity would get the best of her. After a moment's reflection she said she was rather interested in the idea of possibly seeing the man who had done this.

A short while later they brought in several individuals and lined them up against the far wall. I had been told that two of them would be police officers dressed in local garb, while the remaining men would be the suspects. It was evident who the suspects were; they were disheveled, obviously terrified, and one had wet his trousers and robe. (I think I told Hannah he must still be wet from the beach where he had been picked up.) Within a few moments it became clear to Hannah and me that none of the men matched the size, height, or skin tone that we remembered of the assailant. But the chief commissioner was persistent and wanted Hannah to at least indicate whom among the lineup the assailant most looked like. She thought about this carefully, gazing once again at everyone, and then matter-of-factly turned to the chief commissioner and said, "He looked mostly like you."

For an instant you could have heard a pin drop. Hannah had no idea she was addressing one of the highest-ranking law officers in the country, and at first I was shocked at her words, true as they were. But who can fault a child for an innocent and honest comment? After a rather uncomfortable moment the entire room burst out in laughter.

As Hannah's words broke the ice, I glanced briefly at the suspects and noted the flood of relief that crossed their faces. My heart ached for them, and I was distressed that our misfortune had caused such anguish and fear in their own lives. Hannah quickly went on to say that while the assailant was not as tall as the chief commissioner, he had roughly the same build and, more importantly, the same light skin tone. The ambassador and other officials had told me that the incident had become a matter of national importance and that they were under immense pressure to bring it to a quick end. In spite of their friendliness and kindness to Hannah, I got the impression they were disappointed that the lineup did not resolve the matter. By the end of the evening, it became clear to me, regardless of what I said, on its public face this incident was going to be written off as a mere robbery attempt.

Earlier that evening the agents who had been sent to the area of the attack had located the site, noting the fresh tire tracks, the assailant's and my footprints, and pieces of shattered window glass in the sand. After following the assailant's retreating footprints into the sand dunes, they came across a discarded blue robe and a white turban lying in the sand. (All of the men brought in for the lineup were wearing blue robes as we had described, and it was not until after we had rejected the suspects that I was informed the assailant had, in fact, abandoned his robe and obviously slipped back into town clothed in whatever he had been wearing underneath it.) The investigating agents also came across a small plastic bag containing a tattered paperback book, *Petals of Blood*, a well-known novel by an African author (Ngugi Wa Thiongo) that provides a bitter critique of the social injustices and economic inequality in post-independence Africa. The novel belonged to one of Nouakchott's small struggling libraries, and after tracing the novel back there the next day, the police learned it had been checked out by Ali Ould Sidi. The agents knew they had their man, who was already familiar to the police, but his whereabouts were unknown.

Since Hannah and I had arrived at the small clinic, Myles Harrison and several other World Vision staff had worked frantically to arrange an emergency evacuation plane. Hannah still had a dangerous wound, which could potentially cause hemorrhaging in her lungs due to the internal bruising from the bullet's impact. The medevac plane would be brought in from Dakar. We would be taken to Dakar for a checkup, then placed on the next commercial flight to Paris. We knew we would depart sometime that night.

Amrita had gone to our house and packed clothes for both of us in a small case. When she had arrived at the house late that evening, she found an anxious Aboubacar still there, waiting for us to come home for the dinner he had prepared. Because of the tense and uncertain circumstances, Amrita simply told him we would not be coming home that evening.

Shortly after midnight the medevac plane arrived at Nouakchott's small airport. Hannah was taken from the clinic on a stretcher that was placed in the waiting vehicle. I insisted on walking alongside her as they carried her out. An exhausted Dr. Sheikh had stayed by Hannah's side the entire time and now accompanied us, along with a few World Vision staff, to the waiting plane. A few minutes later we were driving across the runway tarmac to the small, double-prop Air Senegal plane.

Dr. Sheikh spoke briefly with the medical assistant who

had flown up on the plane and checked Hannah's intravenous fluid supply one last time while I passed on a few instructions to Myles, who would now be in charge of World Vision's operations in Mauritania. All of us were bleary-eyed and tired. We said our good-byes in the crisp night air and, though exhausted, Hannah graced everyone with one more of her glowing smiles.

I took a deep breath and looked up briefly. It was a breathtakingly beautiful night; the sky was crystal clear, and the heavens were lit with the sparkling beauty of a million stars. I loved this land. There was so much beauty here, and I wondered longingly if I would ever be able to return. In a few moments our little plane lifted off the desert floor into that beautiful night sky. Was this the end of a journey? Was it the beginning of a new one? I pondered these questions, but only for moment. With Hannah resting by my side, we soon drifted into some much-needed sleep.

SOUL TRAUMA

Have I not wept for those in trouble?
Has not my soul grieved for the poor?
Yet when I hoped for good, evil came;
when I looked for light, then came darkness.

(JOB 30:25–26)

I WAS STARTLED BACK INTO CONSCIOUSNESS BY THE JARRING BUMP of the small plane as it landed in Dakar in the early hours of Thursday morning. Hannah stirred briefly as the plane's brakes squealed on the tarmac. It was still an hour before daylight as the plane taxied and bumped its way toward a waiting ambulance on the far side of the empty airport. As I peered out the small window, I noticed the plane was taking a shortcut across a grassy area, rather than staying on the tarmac. Instantly I heard the Senegalese pilot scold his copilot, who had apparently landed the plane, for taking shortcuts while taxiing. The copilot, obviously embarrassed and irritated, mumbled that there was "no activity on the runways at this hour, so why not cut corners? Besides we are trying to get this patient to the ambulance as quickly as we can, aren't we?" The senior pilot then told his assistant that he was being impudent, and we taxied the rest of the way with a rather sullen silence filling the cabin.

Hannah was carefully loaded into the ambulance, and after a quick check of our passports, we were weaving our way through the empty streets of Dakar toward one of the city's main hospitals.

We soon found ourselves resting in a set of twin beds in a small, sunlit room in the emergency wing of the Senegalese facility. Hannah's vital signs were checked one last time by the medic who had accompanied us from Nouakchott, who then turned us over to the friendly nursing staff. After new IVs were in place, we dozed for an hour or two, somewhat fitfully with the strange environment and hospital noises.

Shortly after 7:00 A.M., we were awakened by the arrival of two smiling, familiar faces—Sally and Silvie, South African and Beninese friends who staffed the Human Resources unit at World Vision's West Africa regional office in Dakar. These two ladies had tirelessly labored through much of the preceding night to arrange the medevac flight to Nouakchott and our eventual medical evacuation to France later that day. They were in our room on official business, but you would have thought they were visiting one of their own daughters in the critical care unit. From that early morning hour until our continuing flight that evening, they were constantly by Hannah's side, encouraging her, laughing with her, bringing her food and snacks, and lavishing on her the love and attention she so much needed. While the women tended to Hannah, I had a long and encouraging phone conversation with my colleague and friend Daniel Ole Shani, who was a Kenyan national and World Vision's director for West Africa as well as the person to whom I reported directly.

About an hour later two doctors, one French and the other Senegalese, came in to examine us, with most of the focus on Hannah's wounds. After more X-rays and a thorough examination, they felt Hannah was not in immediate danger, but they were concerned that she could still experience hemorrhaging in her lungs as a result of the bullet's impact. They recommended further evacuation to the Necker Children's Hospital in Paris, where she could not only be monitored closely until she was out of danger but also have her chest wound properly seen to by a skilled surgeon.

I too had both an entry and exit wound in the bicep of my right arm. The doctors removed some of the torn tissue, cleaned the wounds, and applied new bandages and an arm sling. They also recommended that I undergo further examination in Paris to ensure there was no nerve damage.

Earlier Hannah had been given a thorough bed bath by the kind Senegalese nurses; but having declined the offer for the same, I still had a fair amount of sand and dried blood on me from the evening before and was in desperate need of a bath. After sharing a breakfast with Hannah that was brought by Sally and Silvie, I realized I was also in need of a toilet. So I began looking for the men's room.

Unfortunately, when I found the facilities that were shared by other wards in the hospital, they were clogged, full, and literally running over—a big contrast to the relatively clean emergency wing where we had been admitted. I realized that I was going to have to go elsewhere if I were to bathe, much less relieve myself in a way that preserved some measure of my dignity.

The doctors and hospital staff had told me that for my own safety and due to issues of liability, I was strictly forbidden to leave the hospital premises. I immediately conspired with Sally and Silvie to park their World Vision vehicle near our wing of the hospital. They would then divert the attention of the hospital staff while I took my bag of clothes prepared by Amrita the night before and slipped out in search of bath and comfort. I had already phoned my World Vision colleague Estelle Kouyate (my former finance director in Mauritania) and her husband, Souleymane, about my needs and my plan. They lived in Dakar, about fifteen minutes away.

My plan worked flawlessly, and in a short time I pulled up to their house, where they warmly greeted me with a towel, a fresh bar of soap, and best of all, a stiff cup of hot, French coffee! I took a long, glorious shower (all the while keeping my throbbing, bandaged arm out of water's way). Afterward, I felt like I had a new lease on life and could face most anything. Since I could not be gone long for fear of being caught by hospital staff, I said good-bye to Estelle and Souleymane and made a stop at the World Vision office. I met briefly with Dan Ole Shani and had an encouraging moment of prayer, then quickly slipped back to the hospital. Before entering I called Sally to divert the nurses' attention once again while I slipped unnoticed back into the room with Hannah.

After lunch I dozed a bit while Sally and Silvie braided Hannah's hair and painted her nails. I was deeply grateful for the doting attention they had given Hannah throughout the day, keeping her focus off of her present (and painful) circumstances.

The highlight of that afternoon was when my son, Nathaniel, appeared at the clinic. The evening before, Dan Ole Shani had gone to Nathaniel's school and had told him of the events that had occurred, including the plans for our medevac to Dakar. Nathaniel was shocked, but he knew Dan as a caring leader and a good friend of the family, and he trusted his assessment of the situation. He went back to his room and had a good cry. But knowing that the worst was over and that we were now in good hands, he quickly rebounded. As soon as Nathaniel's classes were over in the early afternoon of the next day, a World Vision driver brought him to the clinic.

We had a wonderful visit, and Hannah was clearly delighted to have some time with her older brother. Nathaniel queried us about details of the incident and spoke many kind and reassuring words to Hannah. After he saw we were in good hands and out of harm's way, he also seemed satisfied with staying on in Dakar at his school while we traveled to Paris for further treatment. Later in the afternoon, after saying good-bye to Nathaniel, we began to ready ourselves for the trip to the airport.

Hannah was to be accompanied by two medical doctors, loaded in a stretcher, and eventually placed in a cordoned-off section of a commercial Air France flight to Paris. We put our few belongings in a small case and were driven out to the airport early that evening. There was some sort of misunderstanding with airport officials when we got there, and I was told I would have to leave Hannah and her escort of two doctors and go through immigration and customs formalities.

While they understood that I was Hannah's father, it was evident they did not understand that I was also wounded. It just looked like I happened to have my arm in a sling. I think they honestly thought I was trying to get a free ride around immigration formalities. I was too emotionally and physically exhausted to fight the airport bureaucracy, so I stepped out of the vehicle with our one suitcase and gingerly made my way to the bustling departure area. Besides, for Hannah's sake, I did not want to make a scene or slow the process for her. The airport was packed and hot, and after a long wait in the ticket line, I finally got my bag checked and a boarding pass. I was exhausted, and it had been nearly an hour since I had seen Hannah. I was concerned for her well-being among strangers and hoped she would not get too anxious with my prolonged absence. As I made my way through crowded security checks and into the departure lounge, I was frequently jostled and bumped by those around me. Twice I had direct hits to my already throbbing arm. While standing in the pressing crowd just before boarding, I felt my arm begin to bleed once again from being hit and pressed against one too many times, and I was concerned that the blood would begin showing through my shirt sleeve and cause alarm among passengers and airline personnel before I could slip onto the plane.

I finally boarded, made my way to the back of the large 747, and found Hannah in her stretcher in a curtained section with her two assisting doctors. I needn't have worried about Hannah. Both flight attendants and her doctors were doting over her, and she was enjoying every minute of it! When the flight attendants realized who I was, they were surprised that I had bothered to go through airport formalities and had not just accompanied my daughter! I just shook my head and dropped exhausted into a seat across the aisle from Hannah.

On the long flight from Dakar to Paris, I finally had a few free moments of relative solitude to catch a genuinely restful nap or two but, more importantly, to collect my thoughts on all that had transpired in the last thirty hours. My thoughts were initially drawn toward Hannah. I feared for her and the long-term effects of the trauma she had experienced. Would this scar her for life? Would she spend the rest of her life always fearful of what might be around the next corner? My concerns were much the same as my thoughts turned to Hélène and Nathaniel. Eventually I thought of myself, and I began trying to unpack the tangled knot of worries and feelings in my own heart. As I sifted through these, mentally trying to separate the different threads and determine which were attached to my head and which to my heart, my thoughts drifted back to the moments during and immediately after the shooting.

My first thoughts were of deep gratitude to God for sparing our lives in a situation that could have turned out much worse. For a few moments that are now frozen in my mind, I was certain my life had come to an end and that my daughter's life was also over. I understood with renewed awe that "the angel of the LORD encamps around those who fear him, and he delivers them" (Ps. 34:7), and that eternity had clearly intersected with time as I knew it in those brief yet intense moments near the beach. I was grateful I would still be able to be a father to my family and to continue seeking God's will in the wonderful adventure of life.

But as I sat in the darkened cabin of the plane, alone with my thoughts, I felt something more tangibly human tugging at my feelings. I struggled at first to sort this out. Then slowly the strong emotions I had felt just after the assault came tumbling back to my consciousness. The strongest emotion was the feeling of having been deeply hurt. *Why had this man—a North African Arab, one of the people we had come to this land to love and serve—walked out of the dunes and, without any expression of reason or purpose, deliberately and intentionally tried to end our lives?* What was more confusing to me as I tried to unpack my jumbled emotions was that it was not anger or outrage that I felt—feelings everyone around me in the past thirty hours had either been experiencing themselves or had been telling me I should feel.

Many foreigners will hardly give the time of day to a local

stranger who interrupts their pressing plans and schedules as they rush about their hurried lives in a foreign land. But I had stopped—in the middle of my haste to spend some much-needed time with my daughter and get away from the stress that relentlessly pulled at me in my normal routine back in Nouakchott—to engage, be polite, and even express an interest in this man, his plans, and the events of his day. Why had my considerate actions not provoked even a modicum of curiosity about the reasons behind them?

My tired mind and emotions were stretching reason, but I found myself wondering why the man did not give me the opportunity to reveal my heart, to tell him of my love and affection for his people. Why didn't I have the chance to share with him even a portion of the journey of my own heart? Of how God had peeled off layers of assumptions and prejudice and given me the opportunity to gain a small glimpse of the world as perhaps he saw it—a world where real hope is just a fleeting dream, a place of injustices and flagrant unfairness, a harsh world where fate has placed so many honest and good people in nearly intractable places of suffering, pain, and hardship? Hadn't he seen this through the way I engaged him when he first greeted me?

I began to see that my pain was rooted in not having been understood. In taking the time to engage this stranger for a few moments amidst the sand dunes of the Sahara, I had chosen to make myself vulnerable to him—a decision entirely my own. But the choice was his either to accept or reject my simple act of kindness.

Over the years Hélène and I had experienced the fear of risking vulnerability, and I think for the most part we had managed to overcome it. But I was now discovering that the consequences of taking such a risk could be disturbingly painful, more painful than my physical wounds. As the need for sleep began to contend for my consciousness, I dozed off with the forming memory that even when the man first took aim at me, I had still held out hope he would understand that I was a friend, someone who cared; it was not until he actually pulled the trigger that I fully understood my act of kindness meant nothing to him.

Sometime later I awoke with a slightly clearer head. Hannah was sleeping soundly across the aisle, and I was grateful once again for the insular feel of the darkness in the airline's cabin and the low hum of the jets as we crossed the vast Sahara. My thoughts slowly returned to where I had left off, still replaying the surreal events of the day before and trying to better understand the interplay between my head and heart.

As I pondered all this I began to see how this single choice to act kindly toward a stranger ran parallel to the larger story and choices that Hélène and I had made with our lives—our choice to praise him among the nations, to sing of him among the peoples (Ps. 57:9) wherever he led us; our choice to come to this place and daily make ourselves vulnerable, even at the risk of rejection; our choice of hope that some measure of our actions would reflect, even in a small way, the love and acceptance of the One who had forever placed himself in a place of vulnerability.

We had chosen to make ourselves vulnerable to this land and to its people. But in that moment in the Saharan dunes, in spite of my sincere actions, my vulnerability had been rejected and taken advantage of, and my daughter and I had paid dearly. This choice to love, and the inherent risks involved, had been clearly articulated by C. S. Lewis in *The Four Loves*:

> To love at all is to be vulnerable. Love anything, and your heart will certainly be wrung and possibly be broken. If you want to

make sure of keeping it intact, you must give your heart to no one, not even to an animal. Wrap it carefully round with hobbies and little luxuries; avoid all entanglements; lock it up safe in the casket or coffin of your selfishness. But in that casket—safe, dark, motionless, airless—it will change. It will not be broken; it will become unbreakable, impenetrable, irredeemable. The alternative to tragedy, or at least to the risk of tragedy, is damnation. The only place outside of Heaven where you can be perfectly safe from all the dangers and perturbations of love is Hell.

As I sat there in the comforting darkness of the airplane, trying to examine my tattered heart, I felt the selfish temptation to lock it away, somewhere safe, someplace where life is "normal." But I knew that somewhere deeper still, I wanted to love. I wanted to be able to find the strength, the will, to rise above the turmoil of my emotions and still be a vessel through which the love that had so deeply touched me could flow freely to those I encountered. And I did not want my circumstances, weaknesses, and faltering— with which I now wrestled and which came from this feeling of rejection—to encumber its flow.

I had laid my life on the altar years before when I chose this path. I had considered myself "dead," yet "alive to God in Christ" (Rom. 6:11). How many times in recent years had I reaffirmed those remarkable words of Paul to the Galatians, "I no longer live, but Christ lives in me. The life I now live in the body, I live by faith in the Son of God, who loved me and gave himself for me" (Gal. 2:20). For some years I sincerely think I had come to terms with my willingness to give my life for my Savior and for those he had given his life for. In those lonely hours during the flight to Paris, I began to understand that rejection for caring can sometimes be more painful than the prospect of death. It was not the fear or pain of near death, or simply the rejection for being a westerner in a foreign land or for being an American that was so painful, but the pain of rejection from a people I had come to love.

In the days and weeks ahead, I was to encounter so many well-intentioned people who, as they heard of the events, would say some variation of, "That man tried to kill you and your daughter! Surely you must feel anger. Don't risk being in denial. Feelings of outrage and anger are a normal response for anyone who has been through such an experience, and you need to process those feelings for your own well-being and restoration."

But anger for the attempt on our lives was not the feeling that rumbled around inside and distressed me. It was a simple yet deep, raw feeling of hurt. My vulnerability meant nothing to the assailant, and he had rejected (knowingly or unknowingly) my love for him and his people. Surely Jesus' physical death on the cross was agonizing beyond what I am able to comprehend, but I became more aware of the deep and profound pain of being forsaken and rejected. This was the real trauma I carried in my soul in the days that followed.

6

WHAT NOW?

My soul is in deep anguish.
How long, LORD, how long?
(PSALM 6:3)

OUR PLANE LANDED AT CHARLES DE GAULLE INTERNATIONAL AIRPORT
on the outskirts of Paris in the early dawn hours. My family
and I had passed through this airport countless times in recent
years, and the sights and smells of that place brought a comforting
sense of familiarity and a reassurance to my jangled nerves that
we were far from the trauma and confusion we had left behind us.
After all other passengers had disembarked, Hannah and I were
taken from the plane to a waiting ambulance, and this time I was
allowed to accompany my daughter. Our passports were quickly
processed at an exit gate by an immigration official.

Soon Hannah and I, along with the two doctors who had traveled with us, were speeding through the early morning traffic with

the siren blaring. A half hour later we turned into the entrance of the Necker Children's Hospital in central Paris, and a short time after that Hannah was settled into her own private room. She offered a groggy, warm good-bye to the two doctors after they had finished signing paperwork. (Unknown to me, Hannah had developed a crush on the young and handsome French doctor from Dakar; this did not make the good-bye any easier.)

There was the normal flurry of activity around Hannah as her vital signs were checked, new IVs were put in place, and new X-rays were taken of her chest. A short time later her new doctors came to assess her wounds. After they confirmed that her condition was stable, Hannah began to settle comfortably into her new surroundings—although she was dismayed when told she could not have any solid food until the next morning, following her scheduled surgery.

Having slept under sedation for most of the night flight, she was now alert, smiling at everyone and clearly reveling in all the attention she was receiving. It is not every day that a ten-year-old girl is flown in from a remote part of the world with a gunshot wound to her chest, and on the hospital ward Hannah was clearly both a curiosity and the object of everyone's sympathy.

I, on the other hand, was beginning to falter. I had just passed a second night since the shooting with only intermittent snatches of sleep. Now that Hannah was in safe hands in one of the best children's hospitals in France, I felt the flow of adrenaline that had kept me going begin to ebb. As I sat in the corner of the room watching the whirl of activity around Hannah, I realized that I could finally let go. I did not have to be in charge anymore. Hannah was going to be all right, and I no longer, at least for the moment, had to be a strong person for her sake. I felt my body and emotions begin to crash. On several occasions I felt the room spin. My wounded arm ached, and I was hungry. I looked longingly at the hospital bed Hannah was in. I needed to lie down, pull the sheets over my head, and have the opportunity to cry and grieve all that had happened. Most of all, I need consolation and comfort.

Our World Vision staff in Dakar had thoughtfully called my wife and given her details of where we were to be taken in Paris. The morning we arrived at the children's hospital, Hélène had taken the early train from Calais in northern France, and I knew she would eventually be making her way through morning metro traffic to join us.

Just as my emotional systems started to fail around mid-morning, to my delight and relief, Hélène walked into the small room. I jumped from my seat to greet her, but she made a beeline for Hannah's bedside with barely a glance at me. I moved to her side and waited while she hugged and caught up with Hannah. Some minutes later she looked up at me and without a hug, a kiss, or a touch, asked, "Well, how are you doing?"

Holding my throbbing arm, I gazed at her through my blood-shot eyes, stunned by what felt was a callous greeting after all I had been through. Her evident unwillingness or inability to show affection to me in such time of need hurt deeply. I wanted more than anything at that moment to be held in her arms and to be told that I was loved. I was wrestling deeply with feeling that I had betrayed my wife's trust and not protected our daughter after Hélène had so emphatically warned me a few days prior of the danger she sensed. I mumbled a reply that I was doing okay, and she immediately turned her attention once again to Hannah. I shuffled back to my seat in the corner, feeling like the most dejected and incompetent husband and father in the world.

What I failed to adequately appreciate in that moment was that Hélène, though not wounded physically, was experiencing her own deep pain and trauma—emotional and psychological wounds that I would later learn ran as deep, or deeper, than my own. Hélène, at that moment, had needed me to hold her in my arms. She needed my shoulder to cry on. But sadly, neither of us was emotionally available for the other; we spent the rest of the day seeing to Hannah's needs, yet in uncomfortable misery, each trying to stay out of the other's fragile world.

Later in the day Hélène noticed that while Hannah's wounds and bandages had been seen to, my arm had continued to drain and my bandage was long overdue for a change. Hannah, though, was the official patient. I was scheduled to see a nerve specialist the next day, but at this time no arrangements had been made for my arm. This presented an awkward situation when Hélène asked the nurses if they could also change my bandage, as there were obvious issues of liability and protocol since I was not an official patient. In the end the nursing staff provided us with needed bandages and instruction. Together, Hélène and I cleaned and bandaged my wounds. While Hélène could not cope with my emotional needs, and I was somewhat oblivious to hers, she doted over my wounded arm—and that was sufficient attention and consolation for the time.

While Hannah napped, Hélène and I ate a sandwich in the hospital café. We each danced delicately around the other's sensitivities and raw nerves. My mind and heart were already making forays into the future. *What next? What do we do once this situation is behind us?* But Hélène, true to her heart as a mother, could only think as far as, *What now? What is best for our family and children today?* We agreed that while Hannah was getting medical treatment, we needed to begin devoting our attention to paving a path for her emotional and spiritual recovery. We agreed that we should engage her as much as possible in the events of the past two days and that we should gently encourage her to articulate and externalize her feelings and perceptions. We decided that after lunch I should find the nearest *librairie-papeterie* (bookstore) and buy her a notebook and coloring pencils so she could begin to journal her experiences in both words and pictures.

As I was dropping Hélène off at Hannah's room before searching the streets of Paris for a notebook, a familiar face appeared in the room. Unknown to us, World Vision's international president at the time, Dean Hirsch, had placed a call the day before from his office in Los Angeles to Charles Clayton, the CEO of World Vision, United Kingdom, and had asked him to catch the first plane out of London for Paris to be with us. I stood in stunned silence as he strode up and warmly greeted me, Hélène, and Hannah and explained that our World Vision colleagues around the world did not want us to feel left alone in this time of need. It was all I could do to hold back the tears and maintain my composure.

Hélène and I were deeply touched by the forethought of Dean Hirsch and this incredibly generous act of kindness on Charles's part. After spending some time with Hannah, Charles offered to accompany me on my search for a notebook, as he too thought it was "a jolly good idea" to help Hannah begin working through her experiences and feelings. Charles was a godsend, and for the next couple of hours, we walked the streets of the Paris's fifteenth *arrondissement*, sipped coffee at a street café, and perused a *librairie-papeterie* for a notebook and colored pencils. I finally had someone to whom I could pour out my heart. Charles not only understood the heart of a father and husband, but he was also a brother in Christ who understood my throbbing concern for those we had left behind: our World Vision staff and especially the children and poor communities we served. Charles patiently heard my story, asked gentle questions, and offered occasional wise counsel, but most of all he encouraged me. His presence that afternoon and the next morning was like a balm in Gilead for both Hélène and me.

Hélène and I were given a small guest room across the hospital courtyard so that we could be near Hannah, and we both collapsed in bed early that evening with little said between us. The next morning Hannah was scheduled for surgery to remove loose tissue and close up her wounds. Not long after she was taken to the operating room, Charles arrived with some piping hot French croissants. The three of us enjoyed them, along with coffee and tea in the hospital café; then we shared a brief prayer together and said our good-byes to Charles, who had a morning plane to catch.

Hélène's cousin Emily then took me to have my arm checked for nerve damage at another medical facility on the other side of Paris. Emily, a seasoned business woman living in Paris, had taken the day off to come and assist us, and the drive across Paris— including the negotiation of four lanes of madly circling traffic around Napoleon's Arc de Triomphe—was nearly as hair-raising as anything I had experienced in the last few days. The experience was soon repeated after I was given a good report on my arm and we returned to the Necker Hospital via the same treacherous route by which we had come.

Hannah returned from surgery at the end of the morning, and when she had recovered from her anesthesia in the early afternoon, she was given a meal. For the rest of her stay, she enjoyed a steady stream of delights she did not often get in Mauritania—fresh ice cream, yogurt, and delicate French pastries—which the hospital staff lavished on her. After her lunch that day we received another refreshing surprise. A kind man with a dark complexion knocked on the door of Hannah's room and shyly introduced himself as Amrita's brother. Shortly thereafter a Russian woman with a thick accent, accompanied by one of her grown children, showed up and introduced herself as the mother of Suleymane Kouyate (the husband of my World Vision colleague in Dakar, Estelle Kouyate). All three of these individuals had traveled far and selflessly that day to be an encouragement to us. They lavished gifts of flowers, chocolates, and stuffed animals on Hannah, who was absolutely thrilled with the attention.

We were now well over the limit of allowed visitors for this tightly run hospital, but the staff turned a blind eye to the veritable party that soon ensued. And as the laughter, prayers, and tears filled the once-lonely hospital room, I gave thanks to God for the remarkable presence of caring followers of Jesus from seemingly "every tribe and language and people and nation" (Rev. 5:9)—as the blood that flowed through the veins of those there included Russian, Malian, Sri Lankan, French, and American. Hélène was beginning to feel better with the presence of others who also had ties to Mauritania and World Vision in distant lands. For the first time since our meeting the day before, she gazed across the room at me and, with a warm, reassuring smile, mouthed the words, "It is going to be all right." And I took it to mean, "In spite of all I am going through, I do love you."

Since her arrival in Paris, Hannah had asked several times if she would get to see the Eiffel Tower. Later that night, as I was pacing the hallways and praying, I came to a window at the end of a long corridor and to my astonishment there, only a few blocks away and lit with hundreds of blazing spotlights, was the Eiffel Tower, filling the window with all its glittering wonder.

Hannah had not been allowed to leave her room since being admitted to the hospital, but late the next evening, a day after her surgery, I found a wheelchair and came to Hannah's bedside, telling her I had a surprise. After gingerly placing her in the chair and attaching her IV bag, I discretely rolled her down the darkened hallways to the window, whispering to her to close her eyes as we approached. When she opened them a few moments later, I watched with tears in my eyes as Hannah's lingering gaze reflected the wonder of the scene before her. At that moment I saw once again in my daughter's eyes the zest and wonder for life that had always been characteristic of her. And I felt deeply assured that her love of life and adventure was still intact, and that all would be well with her in the days and weeks that were to follow.

———◆———

Three days later Hannah's wounds had healed sufficiently, and she was discharged from the hospital with the understanding that we would take her to Calais where she could recover for at least another ten days before any further travel. We took the train to Calais, had a warm and tearful greeting with Hélène's mother at the train station, and checked into a hotel a few blocks from Hélène's parents. World Vision had arranged for us to stay in this hotel rather than lodge with Hélène's parents in their small, two-bedroom flat. This would give us some needed solitude as a family to work through the many issues at hand. The days quickly fell into a routine of long talks between Hélène and me over coffee and tea in the morning while Hannah slept in; bandage changes for Hannah and me in the afternoon, which Hélène and her nurse-mother oversaw; and dinner with her parents, after which we strolled the few blocks back to our hotel.

Northern France at this time of year is often cold, with slate-gray skies and a constant drizzle blowing off the North Sea and the strait of Dover. Not long after the initial warm welcome by Hélène's family, we soon found our spirits mirroring the dreary weather around us. We felt all alone in that small hotel room—wounded, emotionally overextended, and separated from all that had been familiar in our daily routine of the last few years. We did not know where or how to begin picking up the pieces of our recently shattered lives. The ensuing days were challenging and desolate as we wrestled with the conflicting directions of our feelings, our hearts, and God's call on our lives, as well as a confusing mixture of advice and questions that came at us daily from all corners of the world by phone and letters. We faced a myriad of difficult questions and choices. What was best for Hélène and the children? Do we return to Mauritania? Is it safe? What about the World Vision program and our long-term commitment to the poor we served? Were the members of the expatriate staff in Mauritania, for whom I was responsible, safe? Should we keep the office open? There was part of us that thought, *This is madness! Just gather your children, go home, and lead a normal, sensible life!* But then God's call on our lives would begin tugging, and time and again, I found myself wondering and then asking Hélène, "After all the years of preparation and service to the poor in the name of Christ, is this really the end?"

While Hannah was in the hospital, people had tried to give us our space, but soon after arriving in Calais, I found myself on the phone regularly with our World Vision office in Dakar; my supervisor, Dan Ole Shani; my own staff in Mauritania; and with other friends and associates from around the world. Myles Harrison was doing a heroic job of holding things down in Mauritania during my absence—namely keeping our program going while trying to maintain a handle on the uncertain security situation—and this was a huge relief to me. But the unspoken question that seeped in between the lines in all of these conversations was, *What do you intend to do?* At first no one would venture to articulate the question directly, but it was understandably the question on everyone's mind.

We learned that the day after the assault, in spite of all I had said to the authorities before being evacuated from Mauritania, the government's official report stated that the director of the leading NGO in the country and his daughter had been hurt during a robbery attempt. This same story appeared the following day in the *Washington Post.* This was disappointing but certainly understandable, coming from a relatively unknown country that was struggling to enhance its image in the international arena, especially in the wake of all the negative press Islamic states were receiving after 9/11. During long-distance conversations we also learned that on the day following the assault, the US embassy had received an anonymous call claiming that, although the attempt on the World Vision director had not been successful, the next one would be. But we also heard that the assailant, who had been identified through the book he dropped in the dunes, had been captured a few days later as he was trying to slip across the Senegal River that formed the border between Mauritania and the neighboring Senegal.

One of the first things we did after arriving in Calais was seek advice and counsel with friends, leaders, and pastors in both France and the United States who had provided us spiritual support over the years and to whom, at least in some measure, we felt accountable. While all reached out to us lovingly and compassionately, we found that for most of them, what we had gone through was so far out of their realm of experience that it was difficult for them to fully identify and effectively engage with us.

An elderly couple, dear friends who had encouraged us faithfully throughout the years, traveled from their home in a neighboring European country simply to be present with us in Calais for a day or two. We were touched by this act of kindness, but in the end, try as they might, it was hard for them to find the right words for us. Instead, they spent much of their time either encouraging us to trust God or updating us on other common friends, colleagues, and related church activities back in their hometown—the latter of which was of little interest to us at the moment.

Part of the challenge was that Hélène and I were each wrestling with distinctly different issues at that time. I was overwhelmed with concern for those under my care: my wife and children (one of whom we had left thousands of kilometers away in Senegal), my World Vision staff, and our community partners in Mauritania. I well remember the elderly couple encouraging us to steadfastly "follow God's will" in all of this.

Hélène seemed to know, perhaps better than I did at the time, that God's will for us was to return to Mauritania. But on an emotional level, it was simply too early for her to get her head and heart around this—and she recoiled at the open and frank admonition from her dear friends. In their heartfelt zeal to help guide us, they did not seem to realize how severely traumatized we were. Hélène and I just needed people who could listen to us, hold us, and weep with us. To expect these kind people to fully understand all of our muddled emotions and feelings was simply asking too much.

Others, especially those we talked with in the United States, told us what faith-filled and courageous people we were, figuratively patted us on the back for being such amazing people, and then basically sent us on our way. But these were not words we would have used to describe ourselves in those days; far from it. In our hearts we felt confused, fearful, and very uncertain.

It seemed that even our own pastor in France, a man who, along with his spouse, had been a source of support and encouragement to us over the years, seemed to struggle with how to respond to us. He had been informed of what had happened, and once we arrived in Calais we expected to hear from him or his wife but never did. I eventually called him on our third or fourth day there. He told me that he had heard our news, and he listened quietly as I chatted. But it seemed our situation was beyond him. He never came to see us in the hotel, so the next week Hélène and I made the long drive to the small church in a neighboring village for the midweek prayer service.

Even then our pastor and his wife, as well as our other friends at church, listened politely and prayed for us, but it was evident that they just did not know how to connect with our situation. While we loved these people dearly, all of this was deeply distressing and only added to our sense of loneliness. Perhaps the most distressing of all, at least for me, was the discreet message from many of our closest associates that since we had given more than fifteen years of our lives abroad in largely hardship posts, it was perhaps time for us to finally "come home, have a season of rest, and get restored." But caring and well-intentioned as those words were, they did not resonate in my heart.

As those long days dragged on in Calais, Hélène and I continued to feel confused, fearful, and uncertain—but what relentlessly pulled at my heart late in the quiet night hours as I lay awake was the love that God had put in my heart for the people he had called me to serve. And I knew with certainty that this was not of my own making; it was entirely his.

———◆———

Many years before, Hélène and I had purchased a small, rather run-down hunter's cottage just outside a small village about a half hour from Calais. Although it had no electricity, over the years this small accommodation with its half acre overlooking the hills of Boulogne had become the place for our annual summer retreats and was a home base of sorts as we went about our globe-trotting lives. There was not much to it, but every year we would find a week or two to add to it and make it a little more habitable, and our children became attached to this quiet, beautiful spot in the hills of northern France.

With all that we had gone through in recent days and with the uncertainty of where we would turn next, it was understandable that one of Hélène's natural responses was to heed her nesting instincts. After a few days of climbing the walls of our hotel room, she began making almost daily forays to the cottage, throwing herself wholeheartedly into a renovation project on that small structure. I remember my dismay when she took me to a used furniture warehouse and proudly showed me a plethora of cabinets, tables, and chairs that she wanted to buy and intended to have hauled out to our five-hundred-square-foot cottage! I was in a near state of panic when I saw the furniture, but panic was not the reaction Hélène needed. I tried to control my breathing and heart rate, and slowly began putting the pieces together while pacing the sidewalk in front of the store. My dear wife was just trying to find "home" in the midst of her recently shattered world.

At that moment my cell phone rang, and I found myself answering another urgent, long-distance call from a government official. Since the incident, I had already answered numerous questions from various security and government officials (Mauritanian, American, and French), and now I had yet another pressing call on my hands. It was not good timing, as I was still trying to get my heart rate to slow, and Hélène was about to put down more money than we had to spend on furniture that we had no place for! The official on the other end of the line explained that he needed to ask me a long string of questions concerning the shooting incident, and I tried to explain that my wife was about to make a terrible mistake that I needed to tend to immediately. He said it was important we talk now, so I tucked my head into the doorway of the furniture warehouse and hoarsely whispered to Hélène that I had a pressing, long-distance phone call to deal with and to *please* not write a check until I was done!

It was clear that the official was concerned that the actions of our assailant could be part of a larger plot. He expressed his concern about the probability of additional attacks from radical elements in the near future. I was convinced that this was not the case and explained why I thought it was only a lone act by a confused gunman. For a half hour on the side of the street, I negotiated the delicate terrain of the official's questions regarding aspects of the political climate in Mauritania and the attitudes of the general public. I tried to convince him that, for the most part, the people of Mauritania are kind, gracious, and welcoming of most foreigners. He finally closed the conversation by stating he would probably need to call again in a few days.

I ran back into the warehouse, apologized to Hélène for the long delay, and quickly pulled her behind a large cabinet, where I said, "Hélène, I fully understand what you are trying to do—and why. But we cannot stay here in France beyond another week or two, and we certainly cannot move into our small cottage indefinitely."

Hélène did not miss a beat. She turned, gazed straight into my eyes, and said, "Well, we cannot go back to a remote corner of the Sahara Desert where they tried to kill my husband and child, can we?"

As the days rolled by, Hélène and I began to find common ground. We both wanted to follow God's will for our lives, that was certain, and our choice to spend our lives together had been rooted in this principle; and we wanted what was best for our children. Hélène was also keenly aware that separating me from the work and call that I loved would only serve to make matters more difficult for all of us. She knew that a fulfilled and happy spouse would only make for a better husband and father to our children. And, to my great comfort, she began to interject this often in these conversations in the days that followed.

———•———

During those days as Hannah's wounds healed, we spoke on the phone with our son, Nathaniel, in Dakar every other day or so. Hélène, probably more than I, thought often about his needs during this tumultuous time. With each passing day she grew more concerned that Nathaniel did not have us nearby at this critical time and that Hannah did not have her brother close by as support. Our regional office in Dakar had already suggested to me that they would be happy to arrange an apartment for us in the city until we could sort out what our next steps would be. Hélène was clearly not at a place where she could face the prospect of taking her daughter back to Mauritania. But as we talked it became clear, especially for Hélène, that moving to Dakar, even if temporarily, would be one step closer to getting our family back together. For me it was also one step closer to what I saw as my unfinished work in Mauritania, and I quietly hoped against hope that we could soon return.

———•———

After nearly three weeks in Europe, Hannah's and my wounds were healing well, although we still had some weeks to go before healing would be complete. Hannah had finally been given the green light to travel abroad. So we boarded an Air France plane for Dakar early one morning after tearful and uncertain good-byes with Hélène's parents, and late that evening we were taken to a sparse but clean third-floor, two-bedroom apartment in the Medina district of downtown. After school the next day we were finally reunited with Nathaniel.

We had some evening meals with him at his dorm, and he spent weekends at our apartment or in town with us, shopping or having a meal. We were delighted to be together again, and I could tell that Hannah was especially glad to have her brother close. The warm African sunshine and the familiar, vibrant, happy disposition of the Senegalese people were welcome refreshment after our gray weeks in Europe.

But it did not take me long to realize that loneliness and the feeling of being adrift would soon set in once again, as they had in our hotel room in Calais. Within a few days it became clear to us that Nathaniel was settled and secure in his school and dorm setting and that prolonged sojourns with us in our temporary accommodations would only serve to disrupt his routine.

Finding herself back in Africa and among familiar surroundings, Hannah began to talk almost daily about Nouakchott, and she clearly longed for her friends, school, and teachers back "home." Seeing how happy Nathaniel was at Dakar Academy with his friends only served to make her long for her own familiar environment she had left behind.

I spent many hours on the phone with our office in Nouakchott, assessing the state of our programs and trying to accurately determine the long-term security outlook. Many of our partners and volunteers in the poor communities where we worked were uncertain and waiting for a signal of World Vision's intentions for the future. It was clear that the situation was still tense and uncertain for some of our expatriate staff as well, and the continued absence of their director did little to alleviate their angst. I worried deeply about my family. But I was also painfully aware of the traumatized staff as well as the communities we had left behind us in Mauritania.

During those days in the apartment, I would often look up from the table or my bed and gaze at the bare walls devoid of any familiar pictures of family or bright paintings by Hélène. Knowing I did not belong there, I would be seized with a deep longing to be settled and for a sense of belonging; the gnawing sensation of being adrift would come crashing in once again. While languishing in the sparse bedroom with little to do one afternoon, I perused a tattered *Newsweek* magazine and came across a full-page insurance advertisement. Covering that page was a beautiful autumn picture of a modest, suburban home somewhere in the United States, and father and children were romping around among freshly raked leaves under the oak trees of the front lawn. I immediately burst into tears at this typical American scene and found myself crying out, *Lord, why can't I have this? Why can't I live a simple, settled life in my home country? Was this all madness—this life of dragging my poor family from one destitute and dangerous corner of the world to the next?* As I gazed at that picture with tears streaming down my face, my heart longed for normalcy, for an uncomplicated sense of belonging. At that point I truly felt like a foolish, wandering, wounded, global vagrant with no home and a suffering family in tow.

But slowly things began to happen in our lives and hearts that brought fresh and needed perspective. We had noticed that some of the other apartment dwellers were Mauritanian. One morning after breakfast Hélène, Hannah, and I stopped at a table where three Mauritanian men sat and exchanged greetings. We told them, "We live and work in Mauritania too." They immediately asked what agency I worked with, and no sooner had I replied than they asked if I had heard the news about the World Vision director and his daughter being shot. I mumbled that I had and eventually asked them what they thought about the situation.

One of the men mentioned that the assailant had been caught, and when I asked what he thought would become of him, he silently drew his finger across his throat—a somber indication of the way in which he hoped the assailant would die. Hélène, Hannah, and I tried to politely hide our all-too-obvious revulsion at the notion of throat slitting. The senior man then spoke, "I do hope the World Vision director and his family will return to Mauritania. It was a terrible thing that happened, and the assailant's actions do not represent the sentiments of most Mauritanians. We would welcome him back, and I am sure all Mauritanians would do everything in their power to assure his safety and that of his family."

I still had no intention of revealing my identity, but Hélène could not contain herself and blurted out, "Well, Messieurs, this is the director himself and this is our daughter Hannah!" The three men sat in stunned silence for a brief moment, mouths agape. Then suddenly they inundated us with questions and further assurances that all would be well should we decide to return. Finally the eldest man rose, warmly offered his good-bye, and said he had to be on his way for an appointment. As he walked away, one of the others asked, "Do you know who that man is?" When we replied that we did not, he said, "That is the Mauritanian president's brother. Be assured, you will be in good hands if you return."

A few nights later I took Hannah on a father-daughter date to one of my favorite African restaurants in Dakar. A minstrel came to our table and asked Hannah her name. He then picked up his traditional harp (a West African *kora*) and began singing a ballad to Hannah. He was being spontaneous and obviously put the words together as he went along, but it was beautifully (if not prophetically) sung by this Muslim man and told the story of little Hannah returning to the Africa she loved. I sat there stunned, with tears in my eyes, as this man who knew nothing about us sang right into Hannah's heart.

As I tried to connect with my own mind and heart in those days in Dakar, I came to realize that nothing had changed for me with regard to Mauritania. I knew God had called us to serve this land and its people for an undetermined season of our lives. And I knew that he had asked us to love its people. As we had done with every country in which we had lived and served, when Hélène and I were called to this place, we intentionally laid down our lives at the outset for God to do as he wished. We had counted the cost, and as far as our lives were concerned, they were his—a simple principle, but one that ran deep. We had grappled many times in years past with the reality that there is risk in a life of service. We knew that under his wings we could always find refuge in our times of need, wherever God led us. But as followers of Jesus we also knew that, as was said of Aslan the Lion in the Chronicles of Narnia by C. S. Lewis, "He isn't safe. But he's good. He's the King, I tell you"—and in this truth I knew that I could find my rest, even in the most tumultuous of times.

Hélène and I talked, prayed, and wept together often. Gradually it became increasingly clear to us that we both needed and wanted to go back to Mauritania. With all its challenges, risks, dust, and dirt, Mauritania was our home in this season of our lives.

We also began to realize the potential impact on Hannah should we *not* return but choose rather to retreat back to the relative comfort and safety of the United States or Europe. She might spend her life fearful of ever returning to the places and peoples of the world she had come to love and trust. And we soon began to see that, rather than brusquely yanking Hannah out of all that was familiar, we needed to accompany her on her journey to recovery in the place where it had all started. We gradually came to the conclusion that as long as we could be relatively certain that we would not be stepping directly and foolishly back into harm's way, we needed to go back and rebuild our lives and the lives of those we had left behind.

On many occasions in years past, Hélène had demonstrated unusual courage, but when she decided we should go back to Mauritania, for me it was the most courageous and selfless act I had ever seen her undertake. And I was deeply grateful, more than I had ever been, to have her as my wife and companion on this amazing adventure of life.

---— 7 ——---

FINDING HEALING IN A HARSH LAND

He will satisfy your needs in a sun-scorched land
and will strengthen your frame.
(ISAIAH 58:11)

WHEN OUR AIR MAURITANIE FLIGHT ARRIVED IN NOUAKCHOTT, THE
sun had already set over the wide horizon of the Atlantic Ocean
that always glimmered under the sun or the night sky just on the
outskirts of the town. Earlier in the day we had said our good-byes
to Nathaniel and to our wonderful, supportive colleagues at the
World Vision office in Dakar. When we stepped off the plane, I
had a lump in my throat as I breathed deeply of the crisp, night air
of the desert once again.

The instant my feet stepped onto Mauritanian soil, I whispered an offering of profound gratitude to my heavenly Father for
bringing us home again. We were quickly ushered through immigration formalities and experienced a warm and tearful welcome

from a handful of our leadership team who had been waiting for us. In a few moments we stepped out of the terminal and headed toward the waiting vehicle.

It was cool and dark, but the night also had a foggy appearance from the seasonal blowing of dust and sand off the desert landscape. As our eyes adjusted to the darkness, four large Mauritanian men, dressed in their blue, traditional robes and turbans, suddenly appeared striding determinedly toward us through the darkness. Hannah grabbed my hand at this unexpected sight, and for a moment images of the similarly clad assailant who had also approached us the last day we were in Mauritania raced through each of our minds. Instantly, with all of my frazzled yet protective instincts once again provoked, I took a step out in front of Hannah and Hélène to ascertain these men's intentions. But before I could adequately react, one of the turban-clad men reached down and swept Hannah off her feet into his arms and held her close while the others quickly gathered around. Hannah was saucer-eyed and stunned but said nothing in that second.

Then, just as the one now holding Hannah in his arms began to speak, I noticed the twinkling and teary eyes appearing through the slits of their turbans. "Hannah! Welcome home! Welcome home! We thank you from our hearts for having the courage to come home again to Mauritania!"

To our utter astonishment we realized these were members of our World Vision field staff, men who had made the long journey from their scattered places of work to come to the airport to welcome us home that evening! As I stood there in the darkness, watching these men of the desert, men of Muslim faith, holding my daughter tenderly and lavishing her with gentle kisses and hugs, I began to see in a powerful way the first glimpses of how God, in his infinite and immeasurable way, intended to bring his healing and restoration to my daughter. Soon their affections were poured out on Hélène and me as well; and for a few precious moments we basked in the loving, healing warmth of our Muslim friends, who loved us as their own.

———•———

As our vehicle pulled away from the small airport, I thought of our years in the Sultanate of Oman, where we had first encountered the important lesson of receiving from those we had come to serve. We had arrived from Africa believing we were seasoned workers, with six challenging years of experience in a Muslim country already under our belts. But Oman has a far more strict interpretation of Islam than that found in many parts of West Africa, and our first months were replete with new experiences.

On some weekends we were invited to spend the day with newfound Omani friends in their homes. Often, and in keeping with local propriety, Hélène would immediately be led off to the women's quarters upon our arrival and I would be entertained in the men's sitting room, with only the young children free to roam between the two worlds. Hélène and I would not set eyes on one another until our departure in the evening.

We soon realized we were out of our depth in Oman, facing an entirely new language, new culture and norms, and an unfamiliar form of Islam. I did well at my job as a professor at the national university, but our early attempts at developing meaningful relationships with Omanis floundered, generally because of our own shortcomings. In the isolation and loneliness of our first months, a caring Omani family reached out and adopted us into their family—having us over for meals, taking us on outings, arranging for our children to play together with theirs, and dropping food off at our home. We were grateful for their kindness; their care and concern touched us deeply in a time of need. But my feelings were conflicted, and my pride was knocked down a notch or two. We were on the receiving end in this situation, but weren't we supposed to be the ones with the answers, the spiritual insight, and the offer of hope? So began the painful process of learning how to be transparent, vulnerable, and needy among those we wanted to help. It was there in Oman that we learned the importance of being willing to be helped and loved by those we came to love and serve.

———◆———

Shortly after Hannah, Hélène, and I left the airport, we were swerving through the erratic traffic and potholed streets of Nouakchott. The sights and smells of the sand and dust, mixed with the chaos of animals (camels, goats, and sheep), pedestrians, street hawkers, and night stands—sensations that in times past may have overwhelmed (or even repulsed) us—permeated our senses with waves of welcomed familiarity. We were home! If you had heard us, you would have thought we had been gone for a year or more. A few minutes later we were pulling into our familiar side street, unpaved and full of sandy patches that often required an aggressive spinning and slipping of wheels to escape from them.

Aboubacar, our faithful house-helper, had been forewarned by Amrita that we were to return that evening. It was already nearly 9:00 P.M., but Aboubacar, who had obviously sacrificed his own evening with his wife and children, greeted us warmly as we stumbled through the door with our meager baggage. Also awaiting us was a freshly cleaned house and a feast—*tchep bou dien*, my favorite African dish of fresh sea fish, a medley of local vegetables, and cracked rice, prepared only as Aboubacar could.

He was delighted to see us all, but his first concern was clearly Hannah, and as he greeted her in his warm and gentle way, I could see he was fighting to hold back his tears. Those who had escorted us home from the airport quickly said their good-byes and left us to our much-needed time to settle back into our own home. Once we were alone—just us and Aboubacar—it soon became clear that he was like a reservoir ready to burst. He needed to talk and unload from the burden of worry and concern he had been carrying all alone these past weeks.

We learned that on the day of the shooting, Aboubacar had remained at the house to prepare dinner for Hannah and me when we returned from the beach. Normally we would have come back around 6:30 P.M. or shortly thereafter. By 9:00 P.M., when we had not returned or made so much as a telephone call to the house, he was worried. We had an ongoing agreement with him that, regardless of our coming and going, he should always feel free to head home to his family before too late in the evening, even if we had not yet showed up for dinner. But that night he had chosen to stay out of concern for us, and it was not until 10:00 P.M., when Amrita came by to pack some of our clothes, that he had learned we would not be coming home that evening. Because of the tenuous security circumstances, Amrita did not feel she could give him any further information. Shortly after arriving at his home, he heard the news from neighbors that an expatriate and his daughter had been shot late that afternoon.

Early the next morning, after finding no one at our home except the day guard, who had been assigned to our home since

9/11, Aboubacar walked the ten blocks to my office to try to learn more from Amrita. But because of the tense and uncertain situation, she still felt she could not give him details and simply explained that we would not be home for a few days.

In the weeks that followed, Aboubacar made regular trips to our office only to be turned away with little or no information as to our welfare or the likelihood of our return. Amrita did not contact him until the day before our arrival to ask him to clean the house and prepare some food for the next evening. And it was not until we walked through the door that he had any understanding of the extent of our wounds or the details of the events.

As we shared our respective experiences, it soon proved too much for him and he broke into tears—the only time I ever saw him weep. The evident love and concern of this Muslim man touched our tired hearts. Later that evening, after Hannah was happily settled in her own bedroom, Hélène and I pondered and replayed in our minds these remarkable welcomes as we too drifted off into much-needed sleep.

The next morning I awoke feeling refreshed after a night in my own bed and home, filled with a deep sense of contentment in being where I knew I belonged. But I had no illusions about the task that loomed before me—surely an arduous route that would be fraught with risks and unknown obstacles. True to my expectations, our return to Mauritania was followed by an intensive and stressful period of assessing security, dialoging with government officials, and trying to answer countless questions for which we did not have the answers: the implications of our return, the future of World Vision's program, and the future well-being of the children and poor communities to whom we had made commitments. These children and their communities were the very reason for our presence in Mauritania. Over the last couple of weeks, I had already heard that many were deeply concerned, certainly for the well-being of my family, but also for the continued partnership with World Vision that for many had become a major focus of hope. And I knew that one of the first tasks most deserving of my energy was visiting as many of these communities as I possibly could.

Then there was the welfare of our expatriate and national staff. While all of our staff had been deeply disturbed by the events, a number of our expatriate staff were still concerned about their safety. I knew I needed to be there to walk through this process with them. On the evening of the shooting, one of our senior expatriate staff members had gone directly to the American embassy and taken refuge there for at least twenty-four hours, so great was his fear for his own life.

Our national staff also worried for themselves and their families, as World Vision was their life and livelihood. Should the assault on our lives serve as a catalyst for increased public sentiment against both Christians and westerners, the staff could be at risk. I knew that in some measure their sense of safety and security was bound up in our own. If our staff could see God's faithfulness reflected in our own willingness and ability to follow his chosen path to restoration, then they would surely be strengthened in the process.

But on a deeper and more personal level, the tension that tugged most relentlessly on my heartstrings was the welfare and healing of Hannah and Hélène. If they could not find peace, our days in Mauritania would surely be numbered.

As a family, while we knew God had led us to return, we still faced a great deal of inner turmoil. Hannah was clearly fearful for my safety whenever I was out of her sight. Every time I headed out the door, she would ask where I was going, who I would be seeing, and when she could expect me back home. Hélène was also anxious, especially for my safety, since I spent much of my days in very public venues. And we both were often awake at night agonizing (frequently with free-flowing tears) over the question of why God had allowed all of this to transpire.

During those days there was never any doubt in our minds and hearts that we were also engaged in a spiritual combat that tested the limits of our ability to resist attacks of fear and accusation from Satan and to continually place our trust fully in the One who promised to be "an ever-present help in trouble" (Ps. 46:1).

I remember well one sleepless night when I was exhausted from feeling constantly tossed between contradicting waves of despair and hope. I longed for our hearts to find solid, immovable ground. Realizing that this probably was not going to happen before sunrise, I began to look back over the days since our return and remembered that, in spite of our weaknesses and the fact that we were often groping in the dark, we had each made progress in the right direction. It dawned on me that, although we had stumbled at times in our failure to trust God to both lead and protect, at least we had been *stumbling forward* in the direction our hearts pulled us. And in the bone-wearying days that followed, when insecurity and doubt seeped into my heart, I would assess the progress of the day by quietly asking, *Have we at least stumbled forward, Lord?* Time and again I would have the deep reassurance that in the midst of our own limitations and weakness, we managed to do just that.

Although there were many among our acquaintances and friends who struggled to understand the complexities of what we were going through, we found that in the most intense moments of crisis or fear, the Holy Spirit would remind us that there were many around the world, as well as those among our colleagues in World Vision, who were praying and interceding for us. Often these reminders came through a phone call, a hand-passed note, or the timely arrival of a letter or e-mail. The communications that encouraged us the most were not those telling us either how we should be reacting or responding, nor those that told us how courageous we were. Rather, it was those who seemed to quietly understand the depth and complexity of what we were facing, and who committed to stand with us faithfully in prayer for wisdom and spiritual combat against the forces of darkness that waged war against God's purposes for us in this land and among the people we loved.

In the days following our return, there was a constant stream of visitors and well-wishers at the office and our home expressing their sorrow about what had happened and their delight in our decision to return. Often they would come in the late afternoon and early evening, so it was usually after 8:00 P.M. before our family could finally focus on each other's needs. Most of the encounters with visitors were deeply touching, especially those that involved our Mauritanian friends. We had true friends in Mauritania.

Hannah was thrilled to be home and especially to be reunited with her small, international school community. In this season in her life, and in spite of all the harshness and even hostility that this remote corner of the western Sahara could at times toss out, this was her community, her world. When we returned to Mauritania, her classmates, teachers, and school staff reached out warmly to her, and she reveled in the familiarity and security of those who knew and loved her. Her schoolmates came from families among the various international and diplomatic organizations in Nouakchott as well as local families, living out their lives in this small desert outpost. Her teachers and schoolmates were white, black, and every shade in between. They were Muslims, Christians, and

Hindus, representing a rich variety of cultures from every continent. Nathaniel had a similar environment at his boarding school in Senegal, and he was right where he wanted to be at this time among his peers and friends.

Hélène and I were always grateful when our children could attend schools that were richly diverse. We believe that as followers of Jesus we are to "celebrate the richness of diversity in human personality, culture, and contribution," one of World Vision's core values. We had always felt that cultural and ethnic differences are part of the variety and goodness of God's established order. And when we found ourselves planted in communities thus endowed, we always rejoiced, not only for the opportunity to live out our faith in such a rich environment, but also for the wonderful opportunities it afforded our children.

Over the years I had noticed among the children at schools such as those Nathaniel and Hannah attended that there often seemed to be a robust exchange of ideas and a healthy dialogue of cultures—a dynamic that played itself out quite naturally and informally. It seemed to me that children, more so than adults, are able to engage in this way without the fear of losing their moorings within their own traditions and culture. Hélène and I had tried to instill in our own children the value and importance of effectively engaging across cultural divides. We had worked to develop in them, from a young age, the will and competence to effectively negotiate multicultural terrain. We had always wanted them to have the necessary courage and cultural dexterity that is required to take steps from the comfort and security of their own customary environment. We wanted our children to be able to successfully relate and learn across cultures, to be intelligent readers of people not similar to their own, and to do so with humility and graciousness.

From our own experience, we knew that effective living and learning in a pluralistic society require effort and a measure of vulnerability; and that, at times, comes at a personal cost. But our experience had also taught us that such competence opens doors to remarkable opportunities and rewards—and we wanted this for our children. At this critical juncture in our children's lives, both Nathaniel and Hannah were experiencing the rewards and support of these rich environments, and Hélène and I were deeply grateful.

Often, when I would get home from work, I would go to the kitchen and greet Aboubacar while he was making our dinner. We would usually ask about each other's day, and we would have a light exchange, sometimes humorous, sometimes serious, depending on events that had transpired. It was not long after our return to Nouakchott that I noticed Aboubacar taking a great yet quiet interest in the way we were responding to people around us, especially to Mauritanians. He was obviously intrigued to know how, as a family, we were going to react to the horrific experiences of a few weeks earlier, and his intrigue only increased as he saw us each day struggling to find ways to reconcile the trauma in our own lives with our desire to demonstrate love and forgiveness. He certainly had a front-row seat to observe our raw humanity. He was there in our home when the stress of the weeks would build up and one or more of us would melt into tears. He saw the fear in Hannah's and Hélène's eyes when a stone was thrown at our window or a stranger would appear at our door. But he was also there as we met with our Mauritanian friends who came by the house to greet and console us, but who often came to be comforted themselves with our reassurances of continued love.

It was not long before I began to realize that the stress of our return was taking its greatest toll on Hélène. I had heard that often it is not always the immediate victims of a trauma who struggle the longest with recovery, but frequently it is the secondary victims— the immediate relative or closest friends of the victim—who suffer the most prolonged effects.

Hannah and I received robust attention from many kind and well-meaning people, both in our native countries and in Mauritania. I was daily surrounded by a caring cadre of co-workers at the office, and Hannah was warmly welcomed back to her school community by thoughtful teachers and classmates who had continued to faithfully provide her with daily support and encouragement. But after seeing Hannah and me off each morning, Hélène was often left at home alone with her thoughts and tumbled feelings of pain, confusion, and fear for hours on end. There were no social venues, Starbucks, air-conditioned shopping centers, or weekly church events where she could find needed diversion from her thoughts or encounter friends and a support network.

For Hélène, an expatriate homemaker consecrated to her family's needs, even in the best of times Nouakchott life could dish out agonizing and relentless periods of aloneness (and ensuing desperation). Equally painful, though unintentional, were the contacts she had with those she often looked to for encouragement and spiritual support. The occasional letter, phone call, or infrequent encounter with a small handful of expatriate friends often involved queries about Hannah's well-being or my own, followed by brief words of acclaim or a pat on the back for how brave or courageous Hélène was for coping with everything. But rarely did anyone venture to probe further, not realizing that she too suffered painful wounds less visible than Hannah's or mine. Hélène and I both found it surprising that many of our closest Christian friends simply could not venture to these troubled places of our hearts with us, while others just seemed to assume that we were strong and coping well. Granted, many looked to us for leadership and strength during these difficult days, and we did our best to provide this as our own strength allowed. But I think they admired our outward comportment, which often blinded them to the possibility of any inner turmoil that we might be facing in our own private lives.

My concern for Hélène grew as the days back in Mauritania progressed, and I often found myself rapping on heaven's gates on behalf of my wife and soul mate for a desperately needed encounter with God's healing touch in those bruised areas of her heart and soul that seemed to ache relentlessly during the long days and nights following our return to the desert.

At the same time I wrestled almost daily with my own human reasoning. Barring one of those seemingly too-rare, direct, supernatural encounters with the Holy Spirit, how, in this remote outpost, could God orchestrate his resources to meet this need of Hélène's? I had often witnessed God's miraculous touch. Time and again Hélène and I had experienced firsthand remarkable encounters with the Holy Spirit that unquestionably transcended our natural experience in powerful ways. But these were days when it often seemed our emotional and spiritual reserves would not get us through to the next day; and if Hélène crumbled, so would I. And crumbling on my heels would be Hannah and perhaps even World Vision's work in this land. At least, this was the sequence of events that beleaguered my mind. Hélène, perhaps more than anything else, needed a word, a sign—from someone other than her struggling husband—that someone in her lonely world understood and cared, and that God had not abandoned her in this seemingly inhospitable land.

It was a hectic, late afternoon some weeks after our return, and I was working with Amrita to get through the long list of waiting tasks that still needed tending to before I could get home to my family when our program director from Arafat came into Amrita's adjacent office and knocked on my door. Arafat was one of the squatter communities on the outskirts of town, where we had worked for a number of years among the endless flood of people who came to Nouakchott from all corners of the country hoping to find a better life.

During the day most of the men and older boys would leave Arafat to seek work or just beg in the more commercial districts of the town, leaving the women and children—drawn from different communities across Mauritania's vast landscape and planted in this unfamiliar and destitute shantytown—with no familiar neighbors or common social fabric. Much of our work was among these women. World Vision's hope was to develop the fabric of a functioning and supportive, if not vibrant, community. We did this by focusing on health, nutrition, elementary education, adult literacy, and microfinance, all with the goal of equipping and empowering these poor but highly motivated women to take control of their own futures and those of their growing families through the pursuit of their own unique aspirations.

Most of these women were members of a number of small cooperatives through which they were organized and trained by World Vision staff to manage small loans for income-generating activities. This income then provided a moderate but dependable source of cash income most often used for school materials or medical help for their young and vulnerable children. Many of these women also had one or more children who were part of our child sponsorship program. For most of them their experience with World Vision's projects had been a transformative one—not only did it bring a sense of cohesion and community building within their disparate neighborhoods, it instilled in them a sense of self-worth, value, and hope for the future.

It was unusual to see the program director from Arafat at this late hour of the afternoon, and without having made an appointment. But he was a wonderful colleague, and I greeted him warmly, asking what had brought him by. Reaching into the pocket of his robe, he pulled out a rather crumpled letter handwritten in Arabic and addressed to my wife. He explained that it had been delivered to him by some of the leaders of the women's groups he worked with in Arafat, and that the letter was an invitation to my wife indicating they would like to host her in the community two days hence.

Mauritanian society tends to be very hierarchical, and it was unusual for community members to organize anything outside of the structure system of local government or even the World Vision project. This seemed to be an initiative conceived, orchestrated, and implemented by community women themselves. I took the letter home that evening and explained its unusual contents to Hélène as she turned the somewhat crumpled and dirty note over in her hand. Not knowing how she would react, I was a little surprised when she replied, "Sure! I'd like to go see what this is all about. I'm intrigued, especially since it is an invitation from a group of extraordinary women." The next morning I called the program director and told him that Hélène had said she would be happy to accept the invitation.

On the appointed afternoon a World Vision driver from the Arafat project came to the house and drove Hélène out to the sprawling settlement of displaced humanity called Arafat. They wound through sandy passageways, dodging people and animals as well as heaps of garbage and the occasional open sewage ditch. A little later the driver pulled into a sandy, open area between hovels where a large, traditional Mauritanian tent had been erected for the occasion—although Hélène was still unsure as to what the occasion was all about.

As she stepped from the comfort of the air-conditioned vehicle into the hot sunshine, she was instantly surrounded by a large contingent of local women singing, clapping, ululating, and otherwise warmly welcoming her to their community as their *malafas* billowed in the gusts of hot, dusty wind. (A *malafa* is a hand-dyed, full-body wrap that also covers the head and provides Muslim women in the western Sahara with a colorful and expressive way of maintaining expected norms of modesty.)

Though desperately poor, with many clothed in little more than rags, these joyful ladies had come dressed in their finest apparel and wearing smiles that were as wide as the nearby desert horizon. Two of the women led Hélène into the tent and seated her in a place of honor on a carpet among the assembled women. Lengthy, traditional greetings and noisy formal exchanges ensued, to which Hélène genially responded. The greetings were soon followed by a round of short speeches by several community leaders, in which they explained to Hélène World Vision's involvement in their neighborhoods and how these community-building and income-generating initiatives were transforming their community and the individual lives of countless women and young children.

Sitting there in the pressing crowd, along with the dust, heat, and flies, Hélène was touched and captivated by stories of courage and hope told by women who counted their blessings for having at least a dollar a day to provide sustenance and help to their families. In the midst of the commotion, Hélène's thoughts drifted back to the events of recent weeks and momentarily collided with the pain she had been carrying. But as she looked into the smiling, weathered, and care-worn faces that surrounded her, she realized that the challenges and fears she faced were truly insignificant in comparison to those of any one of the many women in whose company she sat on that hot afternoon.

It was not until after these short discourses, and some more singing and dancing by these ladies, that the real purpose of Hélène's invitation to this event started to become clear. One of the ladies stood up, quieted the crowd, and turned to Hélène. Speaking in Hassaniya, the local Arabic dialect, with her words translated into French by an interpreter, she solemnly went straight to the point: "Madame, we have all heard of the terrible events which occurred here in Mauritania in which your husband and daughter nearly lost their lives. We, each one, thank God for the amazing way in which he protected them. We are also aware of you and your family's courageous act of choosing to return to our country. And we thank God for this as well."

After each statement, there were resounding affirmations from the crowd of women.

"Yes! Yes!"

"The truth has been spoken!"

"Wallahi!" (I swear by God!)

The speaker continued, "But we invited you here because we too are women. We too are mothers and wives. And while we know the bullets that were fired hit your husband and daughter, we also understand the wounds of a mother's heart, and the wounds of a wife's heart. We know that although the bullets did not hit you, your own wounds must run deep. We want you to know we understand this, because we too are women. And we want you to know that we are here to walk with you, to support and encourage you in this experience in which you too must have suffered deeply. So please know, Madame Norman, that we have brought you here among us to let you know that you are not alone on this journey. We are here with you."

Hélène sat there quietly in that crowd of women as these profound words of comfort, healing, and love began to trickle down into the depths of her aching heart. And then, before the words had fully sunk in, someone stepped out of the crowd, stood Hélène to her feet, and began wrapping her in a beautifully crafted Mauritanian *malafa*. Then others came forward, some placing gold-colored bracelets on her wrists, others placing rings on her fingers, while yet others placed necklaces around her neck. When Hélène saw how these women were giving out of their own need and poverty, far beyond their means, and for the sake of *her* healing and restoration, the protective carapace, which the weeks of loneliness and worry had erected around her heart, began to melt away.

Under their Islamic veils of propriety, as well as the opaque veils of poverty and destitution, these were everyday women living out unique qualities endowed by their Creator. This selfless act of compassionate love that readily flowed across the usually insurmountable divides of culture, economic class, and religious belief was, to Hélène at least, a brilliant and shining example of a people reflecting the divine image—the *imago Dei*—in which they were created: desperately poor Muslim women richly endowed with the capacity to love.

Meanwhile, hours had passed and I had had no word from Hélène. Although I knew a World Vision driver had taken her to a gathering organized by local women, I had no further details. I had been told Hélène would be returning in an hour or two. She had left in the early afternoon, and by 5:00 P.M. I was worried. All my attempts to reach anyone who knew of her whereabouts were fruitless. We had agreed the driver would bring Hélène back to my office where our car was parked, but with the end of the day our office was empty, leaving me alone with my worrying thoughts. I found myself pacing in the office, wondering how I had let her go off to such an unplanned and unstructured event without having better ascertained what was to be involved. I wondered if I had perhaps let my better judgment slip once again.

Just as I was preparing to jump into the car and head out to the sprawling community of Arafat in search of her, I heard a vehicle pull up outside. In a few moments Hélène slipped through the door of my office dressed in a beautiful brown, gold, and white *malafa*, decked with multiple gold-colored necklaces, as well as bracelets and rings on each of her arms and fingers. I jumped up from my desk, took in her appearance, and unthinkingly blurted out, "What happened to you?" She stood for a moment, unresponsive. Then, with her shoulders shaking, tears began flowing down her face. I stood there in stunned silence, and between her sobs, she began to explain in halting words how the women of Arafat had provided for her, in her deepest time of need, what no friend or gathering among her many Christian acquaintances across three continents (Africa, Europe, or America) had been able, or had the insight, to provide. How, in the most unlikely of places, she had found common ground with those who suffer, and how God had touched her heart and demonstrated his promise of faithfulness in a remote land through "the least of these" (Matt. 25:40). Rarely have I ever stood in such wonder and amazement at the remarkable nature of God's ways. Here before me was the tangible, vibrant answer to the cries of my own heart over the past weeks. But never in a thousand years could I have imagined that he would have answered in such a way. And I was once again reminded that not only are God's ways so much higher than our own, but that what we are able to see and witness even in the most remarkable of times are truly but the "outer fringe of his works" (Job 26:14).

I suppose someone could argue that since Hélène was connected with World Vision and the initiatives that were bringing so much help to their community, the motivation of these women may have been selfishly inspired by the desire for our work to continue in these tenuous times. Hélène was no stranger to this possibility. But to her, the magnificent gesture of love on that hot afternoon carried a much deeper message than simply, "Please stay and continue helping us." Their message was one of genuine identity and heartfelt care shared among mothers, wives, and homemakers, each finding common ground in the struggles, fears, and challenges of life. More importantly, through the acts of these poor women, God touched my wife's aching heart in a deep way. I saw my prayers for Hélène powerfully answered as she came away from that remarkable encounter in possession of a deep assurance from the Holy Spirit that she was not alone; she was not forgotten. God brought his healing touch to Hélène through generous acts of selfless, compassionate love by destitute Muslim women.

———— 8 ————

THE QUESTIONS

*Always be prepared to give an answer to everyone
who asks you to give the reason for the hope that you
have. But do this with gentleness and respect.*
(1 PETER 3:15)

IN ADDITION TO THE STRESS OF CARVING OUT NEW AND DIFFERENT routines in a familiar setting, the difficult family adjustments, the plethora of well-wishers and comfort-seekers at our home and office, and the experience of incredible acts of kindness from our Mauritanian friends, the first few weeks after our arrival back in Mauritania were a blur of endless meetings with staff, government agents, and embassy officials. These consultations were largely to assess the security and risks, as well as the status of our program. Their purpose was also to help us set the course for the months ahead, as my hope and intent was to keep our programs going.

But the issues were complex—with pressures, concerns, and questions coming from all sides. I did not want to be foolish and put people's lives at unnecessary risk; but neither did I want to hastily react to warnings from those who were well-meaning but possibly poorly informed, or base our decisions on fear rather than a sense of how God was leading. One thing was crystal clear: these circumstances had forced me to carefully reassess how seriously we took our commitment to walk with the poor. World Vision would generally not work in a community unless it was able to commit to a ten- to fifteen-year time frame, which is the time needed to effect change and sustainable results, and to establish healthy, robust, and safe communities where everyone, especially children, could thrive.

But this was not a one-way street. Although the communities were the beneficiaries of our work, World Vision expected a significant commitment of will, resources, and shared responsibility from communities before committing to a long-term partnership. Granted, the assistance and benefits of World Vision's child sponsorship and community engagement could be life changing; however, it required no small investment for the people and families of the communities where we worked.

Now the tables were turned, and I felt the steady, inquisitive gaze of our local partner communities watching to see just how far our side of the commitment went when times were difficult, not just for them, but for World Vision and its staff. How quickly would we pack up and move away when the lives of our staff, as well as their families and children, were threatened and at risk?

Myles Harrison, the program director for our urban projects and also our security officer, had served as my interim during our weeks away. He had carefully tracked the security situation during my absence and strongly supported continuing. He had spent hours on the phone with the security office at our international head-quarters in California, briefing them on security-related matters. His assessment was a huge relief to me, as I valued his systematic and methodical approach to such matters. Most of our expatriate staff (Canadian, American, British, and Sierra Leonean) felt genuine concern and angst about issues of personal security, but all were supportive of doing what they could to keep our programs on track and moving forward.

On my first day back in the office, Amrita mentioned to me that the chief commissioner for Investigation Services, one the highest ranking law officers in the country and one of the officials who had been with us at the small clinic just after the shooting, had stopped by the office once or twice and had called multiple times in the last couple of weeks. He was anxious to know when we were returning and wanted to speak to me urgently about a personal matter.

The Mauritanian government remained concerned for my personal safety, for obvious reasons—not the least of which had been the anonymous phone call to the American embassy a day after the shooting in which the caller had indicated that a second attempt on the director of World Vision would not be unsuccessful. The government of Mauritania did not want any more unfavorable publicity on the international front.

Within a day or two of arriving back in Mauritania, I had met with the director of National Security. He expressed his pleasure, and that of the government, that we had chosen to return and said that he and his staff would make the reentry transition as smooth and safe as possible for our family. But for the time being and until the security situation was better assessed, he insisted that I should not drive alone, that I should always be accompanied by one of my Mauritanian staff wherever I went, and that I keep his office briefed on my intended movements around Nouakchott and beyond. Moreover, he gave me his personal cell phone number and instructed me to call him if ever there were an emergency and to check in with him once a day. Often, in the weeks ahead, I would notice a handful of Mauritanian men dressed in local attire standing around venues on my day's schedule. I soon learned they were armed undercover agents assigned by my friend the director. On occasion I would greet them and thank them for their service, but on most days I just nodded at them with a smile so as not to draw unnecessary attention. Although their presence was a bit unsettling, I was grateful and humbled that the Mauritanian government was doing its best to ensure my safety. On the other hand, it was an obtrusive reminder of the uncertain circumstances that hung over me like a pall—the ambiguous security situation and the questioned wisdom of keeping our World Vision program going during tenuous times.

My assumption, when I found myself walking into the chief commissioner's office a few days later, was that he too wanted to talk about matters of my personal safety. I could not have been more mistaken. When I was ushered into his large office, ahead of many others waiting in the reception area to see him, he jumped from behind his desk and greeted me warmly, taking my hand in both of his, as if I were a longtime friend. He quickly dismissed the men he was meeting with and told his assistant that he and I were not to be disturbed. After taking a seat across from me, he put out his cigarette and seemed to be taking a moment to think about how to frame his words. He asked about my family, and especially Hannah and me and how our wounds were healing. Then he clasped both his hands together and, with his elbows on his knees, he leaned toward me and began to speak quietly.

"Monsieur Norman, after meeting you and Hannah that evening of the shooting, I returned to my home in the early hours of the following morning exhausted. But I was unable to sleep. And so it was for many days afterward.

"Since that night I have not been able to get the image out of my mind of you and your daughter lying there on adjacent beds. In the midst of the trauma the two of you experienced, I do not think I have ever seen two people with a greater sense of peace around them. And I have not been able to forget Hannah's smiling face and her kind words.

"You see, my wife and I never had children, but I have a niece about Hannah's age whom I love beyond words and who has been chronically ill for many years. She has suffered greatly and so have we. But we do not have the peace and tranquility that you and Hannah had in the midst of your suffering, and I long to know where this comes from.

"How could you and your daughter—freshly wounded by a gunman in a remote and foreign country, among people you came to help—spend hours patiently answering our questions, face a lineup of possible criminals, and all the while speak words of kindness and reassurance to us as high-ranking officials of this country? You told us that everything would be okay and how much you still love Mauritania and its people. Monsieur Norman, where does such strength and peace come from?"

I was stunned. As I sat in the smoke-filled office, with only the noisy rattle of the window air conditioner filling the gaps between his halting words, he candidly poured out his heart while my mind raced ahead looking for the words with which I could adequately respond. Caution bells were also going off in my head. Would a truthful answer put World Vision's work, or me and my family, at further risk? I silently but fervently prayed, "Lord, how am I to answer this? If he is a man in need, genuinely seeking my counsel, then I must respond accordingly, but at what risk?"

As he brought his narrative to closure, I watched him carefully. I could see genuine anguish etched in his face, intersected at moments with unmistakable glimmers of the kind of hope that seems to flitter just outside of one's reach. When he had finished he searched my face as I gathered my thoughts and mustered the courage to plunge forward.

I began with the notion of hope, and how it does not come into one's possession only with the absence of pain and suffering. I spoke of a hope that puts the chill of pain and suffering under its warm shadow. I explained that when he first encountered Hannah and me, we were not without our own pain and anguish at that moment, nor had we been free from it in these weeks that had followed.

Allah is viewed by Muslims as the creator of all. He is both almighty and merciful. But while he may control our lives, the nearness of God in Islam, and being the recipients of his mercy, that does not mean that he participates in our suffering. I gently moved forward, telling him of our belief in a God who willingly involves himself directly with the intimate details of those he created, and who chooses to be personally acquainted with our sorrow and joy, our fears and hopes. I told him in very simple terms that my family and I were sincere followers of *Isa al-Masih*, who for us was the incarnation of hope, the incarnation of a loving God who has taken on our pain, sorrow, *and* sin. It was simply through placing our trust in this *Isa* that we found such peace in times of our greatest need.

When I finished and fell silent, he looked at me thoughtfully for a long moment, then leaned over, warmly took my hand in his, and asked that we stay in touch from time to time. During our prolonged time together, it was increasingly clear to both of us from the growing commotion on the other side of his door that the long backlog of other visitors eagerly awaited his attention. This was the middle of a workday, and his office complex bustled with seemingly chaotic activity. In a few moments I found myself stepping from his dark office complex into the blinding, midday sunlight. As I made my way to my car through the crowds milling about Nouakchott's municipal building complex while shielding my slowly adjusting eyes, I felt as though I was waking from an unreal dream. I whispered a prayer for the chief commissioner, his wife, and his niece. Over the weeks and months that followed, he and I often checked up on one another over the phone, or when our paths crossed, each asked for updates on the other's family and well-being. Whenever we did, he always greeted me as if I was a dear friend or brother.

A few days later the Office of the Directorate of National Security contacted our office to inform us that my presence would be needed a few days hence to visit the scene of the crime with them and provide an on-site, moment-by-moment account of the shooting incident. Our director for administrative affairs and human resources, Moctar, drove me that morning in the same vehicle Hannah and I had been in on that fateful afternoon a few weeks before. It had been cleaned of blood and the windows replaced, but the bullet holes in the side of the car and headrest were still visible.

We were to meet other officials at a small police station on the north side of town, the closest station to the place of the shooting a few kilometers north. When we pulled up in front of the station, I saw that my new friend, the chief commissioner, was there. We greeted each other warmly and caught up briefly on each other's family. I was also introduced once again to the director of National

Security, whom I had met the night of the shooting. We were ushered into the police office to await other officials who were to join us on our trip out to the site of the crime.

As I followed the others into the office, I noticed a Mauritanian man wearing a blue robe sitting alone and smoking a cigarette near the entrance door. He was not wearing a turban, and since I did not recognize him, I presumed he was a driver or some other local employee. The director motioned me to seat myself in front of the desk behind which he soon sat. He produced a small, clear plastic bag containing a flattened lead bullet and placed it on the desk beside a rather large and somewhat rusted pistol—the firearm used by the assailant and the bullet that had passed through my arm and Hannah's chest. I was struck by the size and weight of both the pistol and bullet as I gingerly picked each up to examine them.

Every now and then there was some sort of exchange in Hassaniya between the officers and the Mauritanian man sitting by the entrance that I could not fully understand. He begged a new cigarette off of anyone who wandered into the office, seemed to have a cocky attitude, and spent most of his time cracking occasional jokes and nervously laughing to himself, with no one really paying him any serious attention. But as I listened to the intermittent exchange between him and the policemen, I suddenly realized that he was Ali, the man who had aimed the rusty nine-millimeter pistol at Hannah and me and shattered our worlds.

Since this was a reenactment of the crime, I should have known the assailant would probably be present, and I felt a little foolish for not having thought of this. It was clear he seemed to be enjoying the break from his awful prison cell. Then I realized that none of the officials had bothered to introduce me to this man, obviously thinking that I would not want to be bothered and that he certainly was not worthy of a formal acknowledgement of his presence among our party.

After a half hour or more, the others arrived, and we loaded up the four waiting vehicles and began weaving our way out of town among the sand dunes and under the hot midmorning sun. Fifteen minutes later we pulled up to the spot where the incident had occurred. The police had located and marked the site weeks earlier.

As everyone piled out of the vehicles, I lingered in the background to see how this was going to play out. In a few moments Ali was eagerly offering explanations to a handful of officers and walking them through his version of the events. As I watched and listened from a distance, it seemed he was eager to articulate the details of the events. The picture he painted was that of a robbery, although it seemed to me there were gaping holes in his scenario. He explained that at the time he had been under the influence of drugs that had an effect on his reasoning, so he botched an intended robbery. I made the decision not to challenge him directly and waited quietly until I was called upon.

After about ten minutes the director and the chief commissioner asked me if I would step forward and recount my version of the events. I did so in a low-key manner and was intentional about not making any reference to Ali's version. He was clearly looking for any possible way to minimize the events that had happened, not to mention the serious consequences he was sure to face. He was already in a great deal of trouble, and I had no interest in making matters any worse for him. I actually felt sorry for him. But I knew Hannah and I were not simply victims of a botched robbery. Not that long ago I had watched this man take deliberate, silent aim at both Hannah and me at this same spot.

As I progressed through what happened, it became apparent to those around that I was not making any reference to having been robbed. Someone stopped me in mid-discourse and asked, "Well, what about the robbery part? At what point did he try to rob you of anything or of the vehicle?" I quietly explained that at no point did he ever give any indication, much less articulate, that he wanted something of ours. I explained that I had, in fact, desperately hoped that all he wanted was the vehicle or cash, so I had tried to ask him this—and that his response was silence and a pulled trigger. I made it clear that he had been articulate and deliberate in his actions, and that he had appeared to be very much in control of himself.

As it had been on that night when the authorities first quizzed Hannah and me about the events, I knew this was not what they wanted to hear. I was uncomfortably aware that the official word that had already gone out on the AP wire the day after the shooting was that this had been an attempted robbery. Perhaps the authorities had hoped that my memory would be jolted or improved once I was back at the scene.

As they continued to ask if I was sure that he had never given any indication of wanting to rob me, Ali, who was now watching from the sidelines, derisively interjected, "Look at his size! If I had wanted to kill him, I surely would not have missed. Who could miss such a large target!" Ali was told to be quiet, and the authorities then spent the next half hour taking measurements and pictures of the scene.

As we lingered under the hot sun, I kept trying to find an opportunity to move alongside Ali. I was curious about this obviously intelligent but troubled man, and I hoped that I could learn more. I wanted him to understand that I genuinely held no ill feeling against him. I still wrestled with feelings of hurt and not being understood, but I was not angry with him. I wanted him to know that in spite of what he had done, I would still treat him with respect and dignity. Unfortunately, the opportunity never came to talk to him alone or without our conversation being the center of attention, as he was always surrounded by three or four policemen. I knew from his actions that as long as he was within earshot of the authorities, he would likely retain his defensive, if not antagonistic, posture. While the authorities had obviously hoped that I would at least concede that it could have been a robbery, I think the unspoken truth was clear to all as we pulled away: Why would a man put bullets in a man, his young daughter, and their vehicle if all he wanted to do was steal cash or car?

———— ✦ ————

Another concern that increasingly troubled me was a matter that Hélène and I had begun to discuss months before the shooting. When we were first married and had chosen this path of working among the unreached and poor, we had often talked about how to best meet the needs of our children as they grew toward adulthood in these environments. And we had both agreed that at some point we should give them ample opportunity to establish roots in one or both of their own home cultures. I had grown up with too many friends in the mission field whose parents shipped them back to the United States as young adults to more or less make it on their own—with no home environment with which they could identify. Many of these friends, who were third culture kids, never grew up to identify in a wholesome way with their own home culture, nor any other for that matter. Growing up they were always foreigners, but neither could they fit in with their own culture in the United States, as they had never found their place or identity with their own people.

Hélène and I knew that our two children were being exposed to a rich variety of experiences and cultures that would, at least in the long term, both shape and serve them well as they pursued their own vocations and callings in the years ahead. But although we had striven to raise our children as bicultural as possible, neither of them had spent any significant time in either France or the United States. We had no illusions that establishing roots in their home culture would be easy for our children, but we were determined to make this transition as smooth as possible, largely by being there to walk that path with them.

A year earlier our hoped-for plans for Nathaniel to attend the local French *lycée*, the only acceptable alternative for middle and high school level education in Nouakchott, had fallen through due to unforeseen deterioration in the school's administration. So in the fall of 2000, we were obliged to send Nathaniel to the mission boarding school in Dakar to begin eighth grade. Nathaniel reveled in this experience and opportunity. He loved his school and the rich variety of friends and cultures he intersected with in cosmopolitan Dakar. But we also realized that within a few years he would grow up and out of our home. Being at boarding school meant the opportunities we had to speak into Nathaniel's life were limited, and he did not have a chance to sink roots in either of his home cultures.

So we began to make plans for a transition back to Europe or the United States sometime in 2002, and I initiated preliminary discussions with World Vision as to the possibility of a transfer to one of these places. Earlier in 2001 we had decided that by the end of the year I would inform my immediate supervisor and our local staff of our need and decision to relocate.

But now, with all that had occurred in the past two months and the critical juncture that confronted World Vision's program in Mauritania, how could we tell our staff, our government partners, and the communities we worked with that we were planning to leave? No matter what angle I approached this conundrum from, I simply could not bring myself to make such an announcement. Given the timing, it would surely look as if we were leaving because of the attack on Hannah and me. After much thought and prayer, yet with no clear practical solution in mind, we put those plans on hold and told no one. Taking one day at a time, we focused on articulating that World Vision had every intention of keeping its programs going, and for today we were committed to making that happen.

In the midst of the tumultuous weeks and remarkable events that had followed our return, another unforeseen experience began to unfold. Many in the struggling communities we served had also been deeply troubled by the events of 9/11, and even more so by the assault on my daughter and me. World Vision, along with other humanitarian programs in the country, had found it necessary to suspend its program for a season during the Gulf War only a few years before. With the resurgence of global tensions following 9/11, many people in our communities entertained fears that were unfounded, but nevertheless real—for example, fears of repercussions from the United States government or other Western nations.

But the most pervasive and well-founded fear of those we served in the communities, and which we had to face, was the question of whether World Vision would be obliged to withdraw its assistance, given this latest event that had involved the national director and his daughter. Within hours of being back in the office,

I had found myself fielding questions from field staff brought to them by anxious community members as to our long-term intentions. These were hard questions for our staff, who themselves were wrestling with the same insecurities. So they simply passed the questions up the line to my office. It was at their pleading that I addressed this general anxiety by setting up visits among our partner communities. I began in the first weeks with our peri-urban programs in the shantytowns around Nouakchott and later traveled up-country to visit those in the interior, where Stan and Beth Doerr were stationed and ran World Vision's rather remote Assaba People's Program.

In the years before coming to Mauritania, my time among poor communities in developing areas of the world had taught me the importance and value of being an intentional listener. My work had often involved applied research in water and agriculture and initiatives in poverty reduction. Over the years I had been privileged to spend countless hours interviewing or engaged in discussions with local people, usually farmers, in their homes or at their farms. I started out as a typical researcher, eager to keep to my busy schedule, and at each encounter I tried desperately to forgo the expected formalities of a lengthy greeting and of accepting the bowl of sour camel's milk before engaging in any discussion. Oblivious to the farmers' priorities, values, and time constraints, I usually focused on plunging into my set of prepared questions and moving on to the next "sample" in the survey.

We so easily forget that even the poor have sophisticated value systems, although they may be different from our own.

Moreover, most carry heavy responsibilities and schedules, especially subsistence-level farmers who must often invest twelve hours a day, six or seven days a week, to keep their families fed. As well-educated and comparatively wealthy foreigners, we easily succumb to the notion that we are somehow higher in the pecking order, that our important objectives and busy schedules should take precedence because "we know best." And too often our image among the poor is tainted, and our actions reflect a sense of entitlement and thinly veiled arrogance (in spite of our good intentions).

Many farmers graciously overlooked my rudeness, writing me off as just another ill-mannered foreigner preoccupied with self-interest. Others would insist that I slow down and go through the necessary rituals before I would get an ounce of information out of them. What I perceived as stubbornness offended me at first, but these were the only individuals courageous enough to try to teach me some much-needed lessons on local etiquette and a value system different (and generally healthier) than my own. In much of the world outside of Europe and North America, people are less achievement-oriented and place a significantly higher value on relationships. On days after an unexpectedly long exchange with farmers, I might glance at my watch and mumble something to the effect that there was still much I had not accomplished that day. I would often hear words such as, "Yes, but those things can always get done tomorrow. At least today we have done the important thing and gotten to know each other better."

I was also more interested in doling out professional advice than understanding and learning from their wealth of experience. Only blatant ignorance, mixed with a little arrogance, would cause an outsider to presume he knew more (or better) than indigenous farmers who employed generations of accumulated knowledge to coax a living out of a patch of dry, sandy land in one of the harshest environments in the world. Soon I began to realize that my PhD served as little more than a crash course on principles of science and objective inquiry and that no academic degree could equip me to do what they did.

What gradually happened through all of this was that I learned to listen. Preoccupied with my questions and the opportunities to insert my own professional advice, I always pushed for short, succinct, and uncomplicated answers. But I was missing the larger, more important picture, the larger context into which the answers to my shortsighted questions fit. I sought individual points of insight, but I was missing the story. Slowly, and with the help of countless patient men and women in the poor communities where I worked, I learned the invaluable lesson of listening. I learned that hearing these stories is how we come to value individuals, not just the information they provide. And when we take the time to truly listen, not just hear, we are all the richer for having done so.

I also learned that engaging people in this way sends the message that they have value. They are worth listening to. Their stories are important. This reflects a core message of the gospel, a message of hope that the poor are desperate to hear: that each created individual is of unique value to God; that regardless of their occupation or station in life, they are of intrinsic worth and they are loved by their Creator. Learning this important lesson gave birth, in the years that followed, to some of the most personally rewarding experiences of my career—the long days spent under a shade tree with farmers, listening to their stories, hearing their hopes and fears, and learning to see the world through their eyes.

So, shortly after my return to Mauritania, I found myself plunged into a succession of meetings—mostly town-hall-type events in poor, rural communities, usually under a large traditional tent or a shade tree—listening and giving them the opportunity to express their views and concerns, trying to provide reassurances of our hope of maintaining our programs, as well as answering myriad penetrating questions about our own personal feelings related to recent events.

The first of these meetings, held in one of the shantytowns, is forever etched in my mind. Upon arrival at the venue—an open area between hovels and the small World Vision field office—I was somewhat surprised at the number of people gathered, since I had been told that I would be meeting with a few of the community leaders. Word had obviously gotten out, and those gathered included many individuals who were simply anxious or curious. As I made my way through the pressing crowd, trying to acknowledge the various greetings and welcomes being offered, it was clear to me that there was a palpable insecurity among many, most of whom seemed to be watching me carefully to see how I would react and respond. My attempts to kindly and graciously acknowledge their genuine yet somewhat tentative greetings were met with even warmer acknowledgments coupled with looks of relief.

I was shown to a worn bench in the front of the assembled group, who were mostly sitting on mats that covered the dirty sand. While our local program director welcomed everyone and tried to quiet the crowd and set the tone for the meeting, I sat quietly gazing at each eager, inquisitive face in the early morning heat. With sweat already running down my sides under my loose shirt, I took an occasional swing at the flies that were an unfailing part of any such gathering and whose number always seemed to be proportional to the temperature level on any given day.

But the ache in my heart for the anxious faces before me gave me the most discomfort. These people (who laughed, wept, married, had children, and sought to love and care for their families—just as I did each day) lived a tenuous existence—lives lived on the very edge. Many of them knew, on any given day, the probability that their daily plight could plunge from bad to worse was far greater than that it might improve. And the question I read on their faces that morning spoke deeply to me of their daily search for hope: *Will the news from this gathering today follow the course of our past lives, or will it perhaps bring hope?*

After the kind introductions in the Hassaniya dialect by our program director, I stood to my feet while offering a quiet petition to God for words that would not only bring hope but would also be truthful. Hope, in a sense, is a promise; and promises made are only truthful if followed with faithfulness by those who proffer the promise—especially in circumstances as tenuous as these. At that moment I felt neither strong nor certain about present circumstances, much less about my own ability or strength to fulfill promises about World Vision's future in Mauritania.

But I searched deeper. As I did so, one of World Vision's principal core values came floating up to my consciousness: "We value people. We regard all people as created and loved by God. We give priority to people before money, structure, systems, and other institutional machinery. We act in ways that respect the dignity, uniqueness, and intrinsic worth of every person." And so I started with this reminder: that every person in the gathering, regardless of their station in life or present circumstances, regardless of the times or events of recent days, has value of immeasurable worth. I went on to express how profoundly my family and I had been touched in the past few days by the expressions of concern and genuine love that had been conveyed to us from their community and others across

Mauritania. I gently wove through the notions of tolerance and reconciliation, principles we always articulated to community partners as being core to World Vision's mission, yet I did not specify that these principles also quietly flowed from our Christ-centered values. I went on to share that my family, as well as World Vision as an institution, harbored no bitterness for the events of 9/11 or toward Mauritania and its people. I also explained that we felt no anger toward the assailant or any bitterness for the ensuing trauma my daughter and I had experienced. And on behalf of my family, I articulated in simple, open, and honest terms our forgiveness of the individual who had brought such pain into our lives.

I then went on to explain that while I was still in the midst of intense discussions with those I was accountable to, both World Vision leadership and our connections in various key government ministries (Health, Social Affairs, and Poverty Reduction), I had every intention, *inshallah* (God willing), to do all in my power to ensure that our programs continued. I encouraged them to beseech God, through their own prayers, that he would direct and provide wisdom to each one in this process.

When I had finished, there was a short period of seemingly uncomfortable silence, no one knowing just how to continue the meeting. In those moments I quickly reviewed what had come out of my mouth and assessed its validity in hindsight, desperately hoping it had been, at least in some measure, inspired by the Holy Spirit. I had little doubt that although most of what I said was understood and well received, my articulation of forgiveness for the assailant was entirely unanticipated by those before me and at best was an unfamiliar, if not uncomfortable, notion in this culture. For many it could be seen as a sign of weakness, and it likely flew against most reason and religious instruction in that society. For

Muslims, Allah is all powerful and demands obedience. Weakness and vulnerability are not attributes readily associated with Allah or those who seek to follow his ways. To the Muslim, he is a God who only bestows his gifts to men from the invulnerability of sovereign transcendence. In contrast, the power of almighty God in the biblical narrative is revealed most clearly through the humility of the cross, and in the weakness and vulnerability that were displayed there, as well as in the forgiveness that was declared.

My family's open articulation of forgiveness for the assailant at this gathering and at others that followed was not premeditated. It was a natural outflow of who we are and a matter we never questioned from the day of the assault. While we wrestled with many emotions and feelings (confusion, hurt, sorrow, self-doubt), anger and unforgiveness were never part of the complex, internal equation we found ourselves trying to solve in those days.

What I was certain about was that the people of this community needed to be heard—to be listened to—far more than they needed to hear from me. People at this echelon of society, the world over, are overwhelmingly and exhaustingly the recipients of directives, unreasonable mandates, grandiose discourses, and strings of empty promises. And I had learned that in circumstances such as these, the best I could do was patiently hear their voice and give them the assurance they had been heard and understood.

After a few moments there was some uneasy stirring among the gathered crowd, and it was clear that everyone hoped someone else would have the pluck to break the uncomfortable silence that followed. I wondered if my words on forgiveness had been taken as a curious and somewhat peculiar (if not ignorant) reaction by a strange foreigner who was obviously trying to cope and get his head around all that had happened to him and his family. What

I was sure was milling around in everyone's minds was the still-unanswered question of World Vision's continued presence, and disappointment that I had not come with a definitive answer. For those who live on the edge, simply stating that you are doing your best is often not enough to ease the gnawing angst that is their daily fare. I had tried to bring them hope, but I felt sure that while most understood the conundrum we faced, my words had, in the end, disappointed most of them.

In public gatherings such as these, it is often expected that the women will defer to men, especially those who wish to offer a public comment and carry the discourse. But we had found in the poorest communities such as these where the men are so often absent—tending animals, searching for work for days on end, or simply avoiding the stifling and depressing conditions of the neighborhood and leaving the women to tend the usual plethora of young children in the household—the women are almost invariably the glue and driving force that keep these fragile communities together.

Among many households it is the women who deftly and coura-geously manage the meager resources to keep even a semblance of a safe and healthy home for their children. So it is the women who are also the most aggressive, tireless, and outspoken advocates for the betterment of their neighborhoods. And many of our most reliable volunteers in the community, whom we depended on to implement World Vision's neighborhood programs, were women. Therefore it was not uncommon in such gatherings for women leaders in the community to step out of their traditional roles, fill the void, and take the stand in public meetings, with or without the voice of the men.

I should not have been surprised when one aging matriarch rather stiffly but intentionally gathered her tattered *malafa* about her and rose to her feet in the back of the crowd. In an instant the crowd settled and turned its attention to her, obviously relieved that someone was going to make the effort to muster an appropriate response to my words. The tone of her voice and her dignified posture, along with the silence of the crowd, and even the pause among the many fidgeting children, instantly told me that I was in the presence of a respected community leader.

"Monsieur le Directeur," she began, "we all wish to thank you for taking the time from your busy schedule to come and spend your morning with us here in our community, and we are all so grateful for the work that World Vision has undertaken among us." But without missing a beat she plunged directly into the thoughts and questions that were obviously on her mind: "As you know, we have worked alongside World Vision and its staff to strengthen our communities and make life better for our children for many years now. And we have known all along that World Vision is a Christian organization, although we don't really know much about Christians. But now we see your willingness to do all you can to stay with us when not only we are suffering and at risk but you are as well! You talk about forgiveness and pardon for the acts committed against you and your daughter. As Muslims we are taught that no ordinary person, in and of themselves, has the power or ability to truly forgive such an act. Therefore we are not required to try to do so because it is humanly not really possible. You have even said that your ten-year-old daughter holds no bitterness and offers her forgiveness for this man! How can a ten-year-old forgive a man who tried to take her life and the life of her father?" And as if this were not enough, her last question left me stunned. "Please tell us, Monsieur, where does such power to forgive come from?"

I noticed that she did not return to her seat on the mat, as is customary, but she stood there quietly among the seated crowd, waiting as if to assure herself and those around her that she would get an answer to these pressing questions.

Perhaps the tension I felt in the air at that moment was more of my own than what was really there. For most of those gathered it was probably just genuine curiosity that dominated the atmosphere of the meeting. In Mauritanian society, as in most Islamic societies, any activity that has any semblance of proselytizing Muslims is strictly forbidden. But what westerners fail to understand about many Islamic societies is that there is room for respectful dialogue on most any subject. And in Mauritania there is no law against giving an honest, respectful answer to an honest and respectful question.

Once again, as I had done often in recent days, I silently sent a prayer upward, asking God for his presence and wisdom as I tried to provide an appropriate yet truthful answer. I began by making it clear that my family and I were as subject to the foibles and weaknesses of human nature as anyone else. I explained that we had wrestled with our own pain, frustration, and fears. As in any hurtful situation, we were not immune to the temptation to find our consolation in resentment and animosity toward those who are the source of our pain. But I went on to explain that as believing Christians we had long ago encountered the teachings of *Isa*, and his words and the truth found in them had impacted our lives in a profound way. Our encounter with his love, not only for us, but for all people, is the very reason we made our lives in Mauritania and the reason for World Vision's work among the poor. Through faith in him we find that we are endowed with *Isa*'s love for those we walk among, both the good and the bad. And as followers of *Isa*, and through our experience of his mercy in our own brokenness, we find the power to forgive—born of a love whose source is truly beyond ourselves.

My remarks were soon followed by warm comments from many others, as well as words of gratitude for our love and courage in the midst of hardship. We talked more about World Vision's program in their community, and I was able to answer a number of practical questions about our hopes and intentions. Before the meeting concluded, many publicly assured me of their prayers that God would guide and protect World Vision during these difficult times.

This was surely one of the most remarkable meetings I had attended since I first set foot in Mauritania, and it was followed by many similar meetings with similar questions as I traveled around the country, visiting our partner communities. The reactions and questions these meetings and my words generated took us by surprise. On multiple occasions I found myself having to publicly answer questions about our Christian faith and where we found this power and strength to forgive, much less return to a country where we had experienced such harm. Within a few days one of the local Arabic papers carried the news that we had forgiven the assailant, and it was only then that we began to understand more fully the import of our actions.

The legal system of Mauritania is a mix of colonially inherited French civil law and Islamic *sharia* law, the latter of which generally calls for the death penalty for those who unjustly take the life of another—a penalty that can only be revoked by the victim or the victim's immediate family. While Ali had not succeeded in taking our lives, the consequences of his actions were clearly dire—at least in the minds of most Mauritanians we encountered. And a public articulation of forgiveness by those he had attempted to kill would surely reduce (in a significant way) the severity of the consequences he would face should his case ever come to court. Unexpectedly, our actions had provoked a flood of questions, both private and public—questions whose answers were at the very core of our reason for being in this country, but about which, under normal circumstances, we could never share publicly due to the restrictions of our adopted country. Doors of opportunity began to open as we sought ways to appropriately answer these questions, to share the reason for the hope that is within us (1 Peter 3:15), and to tell the story of the One who is the source of that hope. As a result of these moving encounters with those we served and the ensuing reactions, my staff and I gradually began to see how God, in his infinite wisdom, had taken personal tragedy and used it in direct answer to our prayers.

In the midst of these remarkable meetings with our partner communities, my senior Mauritanian staff approached me with another matter. During the past seventeen years of World Vision's work in this country, we had never been invited, nor had the opportunity, to meet with the Mauritanian president, Maaouya Ould Sid'Ahmed Taya. Other mainline humanitarian organizations, such as those affiliated with the United Nations and other secular institutions, had been invited in times past to brief the president on their work. Throughout the years World Vision had grown to be the nation's largest NGO. Among the NGOs in Mauritania, we were now the government's primary partner in implementing its poverty-reduction strategy; we were the principal implementer of the UN World Food Program's food distribution initiative; and we were actively engaged in the largest number of needy, rural, and urban communities across the country. At the same time, we were an openly Christian organization operating in an Islamic republic, and there were still many individuals and interest groups who questioned whether such an organization should be allowed to continue its work in Mauritania.

Our senior staff had learned informally that, given recent events, President Taya would probably be open to an audience with me. I felt it was important that we seize this opportunity to brief him on both our ethos and on the active role World Vision played in reducing poverty and enhancing the lives of Mauritania's children.

Two weeks later I was driven to the presidential palace. After a few formalities and a short wait, I was escorted into a sitting room where the president himself genially greeted me. I had often seen his image in the newspaper or on local television, and he seemed to split his public time equally between a traditional Mauritanian robe and a smart suit and tie. On this day he had donned a dark, western-style suit. He was rather short of stature and sported a large, black mustache that seemed to match his dark, flashing eyes. I was surprised, although pleased, when he addressed the handful of advisors in the room and asked that he and I be left alone for this visit.

He offered me the seat adjacent to him and immediately asked about me and my family, and especially my daughter, and offered sincere condolences for what had transpired. He said he had been informed the incident appeared to have been an attempted robbery, and he was obviously surprised when I apologized and hesitantly told him that, in fact, the events I experienced had given no indication, at least to me, that robbery was the motive. This revelation moved him quickly to the topic that I soon learned was foremost on his mind—the perceptions of Americans and those in other Western nations with regard to Mauritania and its people in the aftermath of both 9/11 and the recent attack on Hannah and me. He asked me, in a rather circumspect way, how I felt others might view his country given these circumstances.

I had come to this meeting hoping to have the opportunity to provide the president with a clear and transparent briefing on

World Vision and its work in his country, and most importantly the unique way we went about engaging communities through our child-focused approach. Although he was the president, I had been informed by some of my national staff that the full import of World Vision's history of humanitarian work in Mauritania was probably not well known by him. There were certainly those who preferred that the successes of a Christian organization not be given what they considered to be undue attention. So President Taya's preoccupation with outside perceptions, as well as his direct questions, caught me somewhat off guard. I knew my time with him was limited, and my mind raced as to how I could turn the conversation around.

I chose to plow forward. "Monsieur le Président, I can only speak in generalities about others' perceptions, but I can speak with certitude about my own perceptions as an American who has lived and worked closely among Mauritanians in recent years. I, for one, consider it a privilege to work among the Mauritanian people and have found them to be generous and welcoming, especially among the very poor communities where I spend most of my time. The people's courage and commitment to seeking a better life for their families have been deeply inspiring and personally transforming for me.

"Not only has World Vision had the opportunity to serve and assist these communities, but many remarkable individuals we have encountered in this journey have also spoken into our own lives, and we are all the more enriched for it. More importantly, the expression of love and concern by these very people in the aftermath of the attack on Hannah and me has been nothing short of overwhelming. My family, Monsieur le Président, has been indelibly impacted for the good by your people."

He gazed at me for a moment with a very surprised and quiz-zical look.

"I am pleased that you feel this way, especially after all that has happened to you and your family. Do you think there are others in America and Europe who, like you, may not view us so critically?"

I replied that I saw no reason why they should view Mauritania critically and went on to share that few places on earth are immune to individual acts of violence and that I still considered Nouakchott a much safer place to live than many cities in Europe or the United States. Then I continued, "As an American I have always articu-lated my admiration for your people, and recent events have not changed my perspective. If anything, the outpouring of love my family has received in recent months has only served to confirm those convictions."

He seemed greatly relieved by this comment of mine. I sincerely think he had expected me to be somewhat bitter and resentful, and to make demands for better protection for our staff. But after this comment he thanked me for my perspective and assured me that he was doing all in his power to ensure safety and security in Mauritania during these tumultuous times.

He then seemed ready to move the conversation in the direction I had been trying to steer it. I presented him with a folder of docu-ments and photos concerning World Vision's program and quickly reviewed its seventeen-year history in Mauritania, as well as the status of our present programs in health, education, literacy, micro-finance, agriculture, and food aid. He was obviously impressed and said that he had not realized how much we were doing. I then took the next step, and in our remaining minutes gently unpacked our ethos and core values as a Christian organization, driving home the point—as I had done during my recent community visits—that "we value people," all people: the rich and the poor, the strong and the weak. And that because the poor and the weak are valued the least by most people and societies, World Vision chooses to identify with them and walk alongside them on a journey of hope.

The president listened thoughtfully and was clearly intrigued. He expressed his gratitude for having had this opportunity to learn so much about World Vision's work. Then he thanked me warmly, and my twenty-minute audience with him was over.

9

THE IMAM'S REMARKABLE COUNSEL

For Christ's love compels us.
(2 Corinthians 5:14)

THE GENEROUS OUTPOURING OF LOVE AND CONCERN WE RECEIVED, along with the remarkable opportunities to answer pointed and poignant questions, touched us deeply. Each day we continued to marvel not only at the way God demonstrated his care for us but at the ways in which our suffering had opened such unexpected doors of opportunity. Sandstorms in the Sahara can blow in suddenly and fiercely, leaving the once-clear blue skies and open spaces filled with a lingering pallor that erases all shadows and removes the edges from all things. But they clear ever so slowly, almost imperceptibly, sometimes taking days if there is no rain to clean the skies. We came to see that, with the same subtlety that gradually brings back the edges and contours of life after a sandstorm, the

Holy Spirit had indeed been audaciously answering our petitions of months, even years, that he would open doors of opportunity for those we quietly served to hear and observe the ways of a living, powerful, and caring heavenly Father.

My concern for the safety and well-being of both our expatriate and national staff continued to weigh on me. But I wrestled more deeply with the matter of our commitment to the poor of Mauritania. How could we leave them when their lives were already bordering on hopelessness? What kind of witness would it be for Christ and his love for all people if we abandoned these people we had come to serve in their own time of need? Yet each day I faced conflicting advice from multiple directions and from many I respected deeply—our local World Vision staff, World Vision leadership in our international office, our government partners in Mauritania, the communities we served, and friends, family, and pastors around the world to whom we felt accountable in some measure.

Our Mauritanian friends and colleagues in the government and in the communities where we worked were well aware of the tenuous circumstances. But they consistently beseeched us to keep our hands to the plow and weather this period, which would hopefully soon pass. My many colleagues in World Vision were all over the map on the question. Some encouraged us to stay put while others, especially those who had little firsthand experience of Mauritania, stressed the risks of maintaining an expatriate team in such a potentially hostile environment. One even went so far as to insinuate that the blood of my staff would be on my hands if anything should happen to them. This notion, of course, was distressing.

My immediate supervisor, Dan Ole Shani, with whom I was on the phone constantly during those days, was a reassuring source of balanced wisdom and advice. In the midst of serving as a helpful sounding board, he consistently reminded me of World Vision's general position on such matters: that while dialogue with World Vision leadership and our international security personnel was an important resource for making such decisions, at the end of the day, the national director of each field program called the final shot on decisions such as these.

On the one hand I was grateful those of us who lived closest to the situation, and whose lives would be most affected by a decision, would be allowed to own it. But at other times I wished that someone else could, or would, take up the burden and make the decision for me. Our local staff provided wonderful support, anxious as many of them were. In the end they agreed that the decision was mine and generously gave me both the support and space I needed to assess and work through the complexities of such a decision.

My greatest struggle at this time was perhaps with those I felt accountable to spiritually. First, on a personal level, were my wife and children. Although we were all deeply touched by the unexpected outpouring of love and support we found in Mauritania, we still wrestled with the conflicting matters that raged between our heads and hearts. Frankly, there were days (and many sleepless nights) when we just wanted out of it all. We wanted stability, sanity, and a reasoned life; and everything we were doing in Mauritania seemed to scream out in contrast to these reasoned notions in our heads. I relied heavily on Hélène's sense of call and purpose in all that we set our hearts to, and had done so from the first days of our marriage. But when I saw her struggle with her own emotional and spiritual capacity, I struggled too. Nathaniel was a source of welcomed stability. He trusted us to follow God's call on our hearts. At this stage, his life was willingly attached to what we felt was right. Hannah was just glad to be back home and among friends.

She yearned for stability and all that was familiar. But she was also deeply affected by our struggles, much as we tried to insulate her from our more trying moments.

Another great concern was that our friends and pastors back in Europe and the United States, who had been an important source of moral and spiritual support for us over the years, did not understand how their comments to us could put us and our work in danger. During our recent weeks in France for Hannah's recovery, I had called and consulted with a number of them, but continuing the dialogue from Mauritania was difficult at best. We had to be cautious with what was said during phone calls or through electronic mail. Only a few months earlier a colleague working for a secular NGO had been expelled from the country for a politically charged e-mail he had sent to a friend abroad. Because of this, it was nearly impossible to fully articulate to these friends the questions that weighed on my heart.

Many of them found it difficult to appreciate the communication constraints (and risks) we worked under in Mauritania. A carefully worded question on my part could be (and often was) answered with starkly open and rather careless language. At the same time, Hélène and I had both learned years before that it was unrealistic to expect these people, dear as they were, to fully understand the unusual complexities and nuances of our lives in the parts of the world we often frequented. In the midst of these sporadic and cautious dialogues, many of them gave us the impression that we should question the notion of staying on, and that wisdom would perhaps dictate that after more than fifteen years of living and working in Muslim countries, it was now time for us to come home to heal, get refreshed, and be restored.

This reasoning tugged painfully at our hearts. It struck a

deep cord of yearning for home—and I have little doubt it was tied to the normal, deeper yearning for a permanent home, the New Jerusalem, a lifelong desire to finally be in the "courts of . . . the living God" (Ps. 84:2). There were certainly times when this yearning and tugging made sense in my head and would pull me in the direction of my cultural "home"—the security of America or Europe, family, friends, familiar churches, the house I dreamed of in suburban America with the oak trees and autumn leaves. But my heart ached for those in Mauritania, and I needed wisdom to know how to come to terms with these competing desires.

This question, this conundrum, was my daily fare and the inner struggle I faced. And it continued to weigh heavily on my head and heart throughout each day, when I went to bed at night, and in the lonely night hours when I would awake from shallow sleep. I desperately needed to put this question to rest so that we could move forward with the many urgent and pressing tasks at hand, unhindered by fear and doubt. I wanted to follow God's call on my heart and Hélène's. I wanted to be responsible to my family and their needs. I wanted to honor the commitments we had made to the Mauritanian people. I wanted to respect the wisdom of our colleagues in the Mauritanian government. I wanted to honor those we had accountability to spiritually. And I yearned for the safety and well-being of our staff. But I could not put the pieces together. I needed to hear from God.

Then one morning while at the office, and seemingly unconnected to this constant tension between my head and heart and my prayer for resolution, it came to me—a quiet yet pressing thought, a need: *I should try to make contact with a leading imam.* At the time I never connected this with a possible answer to my prayers. It just came to me as an incredibly wise thing to do. Why not try to get an audience with one of the leading Muslim clerics to get his take on all that was going on? I pondered this during the morning, then asked Amrita to arrange a meeting in the next day or two with my senior staff who were in Nouakchott at the time—as many were often on the road or working in up-country sites.

As she went to work on this, I found myself wondering why I had never thought of talking to one of these clerics earlier in my time here in Mauritania. For the most part only the occasional Mauritanian staffer would engage a local cleric from time to time, usually on sticky matters that concerned a local community. But in my time as director, I could not recall any of the expatriate team intentionally meeting with any senior clerics on big-picture matters that we dealt with as a major relief and development institution in Mauritania. I think our general attitude (including that of many of our Mauritanian staff) was to try to keep a low profile on the religious front so as to avoid unnecessary attention and potential detractors of our program (as I am sure there were among Mauritania's clerics). But the more I pondered this, I realized this oversight was really to our shame, and we should have been more intentional about quietly seeking more constructive engagement. Now that there was a crisis on hand, it made sense to me.

A day or two later I met with a handful of our senior staff, mostly Mauritanians, and reiterated the challenge of determining the pros and cons of maintaining the program for the present. My heart's pull to stay the course was certainly winning the day, and I shared as much. I also knew that everyone in that room felt the same. But I wanted to be sure this was what we should do. And I felt it prudent that we should consult all who could speak into this matter.

I put the idea on the table that perhaps I should speak with one of the imams and asked my senior staff if they would support the idea and help with the arrangements. Within a few minutes I knew I had their unanimous support, but suggested I give them a day or two to make some quiet inquiries and get back to me. Two days later I received a call from one of the staff members who said he had just received news that one of Nouakchott's prominent clerics, a man who had some knowledge of World Vision's work, had agreed to see me. Moreover, the imam had clearly indicated that he would meet me at my office! I was both surprised and delighted that he had so readily agreed to grant me an audience, but I was shocked that he would come to World Vision's office complex. I quickly challenged this notion as we talked on the phone, but was told that this was the cleric's clear request. A visit to my office would, of course, be a great honor, but I knew that it was a highly unusual gesture for a man of his stature in this society, and I did not want him taking any risks on my behalf or World Vision's.

Amrita found the number for the imam's office. I called and explained to his staff that I was delighted he had agreed to see me, but would they please communicate to him that I would be more than happy to meet him at his office or even at the mosque—any place of his preference. The man on the line politely but firmly replied, "Monsieur Norman, the imam has given very clear instructions that he would like to meet you at *your* office, and he will be there tomorrow at 10:00 A.M. I think we should best leave it at that." With the clarity of that reply, I could only agree.

Around 10:00 A.M. the next morning, there was a small commotion outside, and Amrita informed me that the imam was arriving. I glanced out the door from my second-floor office and saw two young men gently assisting the elderly man up the stairs. He was a slight, light-skinned man, dressed in a long, white robe and a matching turban wrapped around his head and neck. His long, white beard matched his clothing, and indeed gave him the aura of a wizened sage. But his sharp, clear eyes had maintained their youthful look, and it was obvious that they missed little. As the men moved through Amrita's reception office and into mine, Amrita whispered her assurances that she would be at work praying for us (as I always knew she did for meetings such as these) during this special encounter.

When the imam and his two assistants entered my office, we shook hands politely and exchanged brief formalities before we all took our seats. I had asked Ahmed, one of my senior Mauritanian program managers, to join us, since he had met the imam a few times in the past. I wanted to keep the meeting as small as possible, but I felt it important to have at least one of my Mauritanian colleagues with me so that he could report the meeting outcomes directly back to his own colleagues—although I had no idea what to expect of this meeting, much less the results. In many ways I felt I was groping in the dark, but I was certain that this was the right thing to do at this time. Once seated, I again welcomed him and thanked him for coming to my office. He responded softly but with impeccable French, expressed his condolences about the horrific incident, his repulsion for the thoughtless acts of the assailant, and then inquired about my recovery and Hannah's.

He was clearly a reflective person and not given to many words. And, unknown to me at the moment, this man in a short time would be elected president of the Ulama—the leading body of Islamic clerics and scholars in the country. Under normal conditions, expected formalities in Mauritanian culture in such a meeting would call for rather lengthy greetings and exchanges about one's health and work. It would be considered improper, even rude, to jump into the issues at hand after a brief hello, as

Americans are prone to do (and often even without the hello). So after his brief words there was an uncomfortable moment of silence, as I was unsure how to proceed with the delicate matter that was foremost in my mind.

After a moment of hesitation I cleared my throat and plowed in. "Sir, we are both aware of the uncomfortable circumstances of past months that brought me to the place of requesting an audience with you. But for the sake of our time and the importance of the matters, and with your permission, would you allow us to dispense with expected formalities and go directly to the issues at hand?" To my relief he did not seem offended by this and simply nodded his head slightly in affirmation, without uttering a word. I continued, "As you know, World Vision is a Christian organization that has worked in your country for some seventeen years now. And we have considered it a privilege to be able to serve the people of your country during this time. But Mauritania is also an Islamic republic, and I can understand how there are those who find it difficult to accept the presence of a Christian organization working among so many vulnerable, Muslim communities.

"I'm sure you are also aware of the challenges World Vision and other foreign organizations faced during the Gulf War. And we both know the impact the events of 9/11 and the recent shooting have had on the political climate and security concerns for westerners and especially for a Christian organization such as ours.

"But, sir, here is my quandary. We have made commitments to the communities we work with, as they have with us, and we take these commitments seriously. And I am extremely hesitant to abandon our service to poor communities where so many count on us to walk with them on their journey to a future more secure and hopeful. My staff, both expatriate and Mauritanian, feel it is important we continue the program without interruption, if at all possible. But there are those who feel it is unwise, even within my own organization, and especially those I am accountable to spiritually, including my pastors and others I look to for spiritual guidance.

"Some tell me it is unwise to put others at risk, even if I personally am willing to take that risk, while others tell me that I have rendered my service, and it is time to return home to heal and restore. So I am torn. I am at a crossroads, and I do not know which way to turn. This is why I wanted to speak with you. Please, sir, would you share with me your wisdom and counsel on this matter?"

Ahmed, who had been sitting there quietly watching this encounter, was now staring at me, mouth agape. He well understood the security challenges and the difficult decisions we faced, but he was clearly surprised to hear me share my own inner, spiritual struggles as a Christian with a Muslim cleric. In the following silence Ahmed, somewhat belatedly, gathered himself and turned to the imam to hear his response. It was at this moment that the longest, and the most discomforting, silence ensued.

The imam stared at the ground for what seemed like endless seconds. Then he reached his finger under his turban and slowly scratched his head reflectively and let out a long, slow sigh. The unspoken message I thought I was hearing by his silent actions was something to the effect of, "Monsieur Norman, the answer to your question is so self-evident, need I even bother with a response?" But I could not have been more mistaken.

After another long moment of reflection, the imam finally turned his gaze to me and quietly said, "Monsieur Norman, there are three things I think you need to know. First, your staff who work among our communities are well trained and effective, and their professionalism is commendable. Second, when World Vision comes into our poor communities, you bring a wholesome sense of order to these destitute places, where there is so much uncertainty and often so much upheaval. Both of these aspects of World Vision's work are truly commendable." Then he shook his bony index finger at me for emphasis and continued. "But there is a third matter, Monsieur Norman, which I think you may not fully understand." By this point my heart was racing, as I was again sure the hatchet was going to fall, certain he would say, "Nevertheless, a Christian organization working among devout Muslims is simply not compatible." But his next words shocked me.

He said softly, "You see, Monsieur Norman, we Muslims give alms and help the poor because the Quran instructs us to do so." I supposed the imam was referring to *zakat*, one of the five pillars of duty in Islam, in which believers are required to give a certain percentage of their income to the poor and needy (the other pillars being the affirmation that there is but one God and Mohammed his prophet, ritual prayer five times daily, fasting in the month of Ramadan, and the once-in-a-lifetime pilgrimage to Mecca for those who are able). He continued, "This is an obligation. But with World Vision, you work with the poor *because you love the poor*. This is different. This is what sets you apart. If for no other reason, I encourage you to stay in this country and teach our people how to love their poor."

I was astounded by his unexpected words. I glanced quickly at Ahmed, whose eyes were glued to the imam with a look of astonishment that barely surpassed my own. In that moment much of the confusion and torment of my heart seemed to evaporate, and God's purpose and will began to shine through with refreshing clarity. As I stared quietly at the imam, a stream of thirst-quenching assurance flooded the depths of my soul. His words were not only needed confirmation about the importance of continuing our programs, but in a time of great personal doubt about our effectiveness in this restricted country, they were also a confirmation that our work was having its hoped-for impact.

In that moment I saw that God had all along been answering our cry to him that we would be effective vessels of his love in this harsh land. I also saw that, in spite of the huge gulfs that might separate us, there was much more room for common ground, for mutual understanding and assistance, and incredible, untapped opportunities for Christians to work together with Muslim friends for the cause of the poor that Christ places on our hearts.

The fresh period of awkward silence that followed was entirely of my own making. I was so stunned that I stumbled for the right words. I eventually gathered my wits and somewhat haltingly told the imam that I could hardly find the words to respond to his gracious comments. I told him how humbling and comforting his words were for me, as well as for all of my staff, both Christian and Muslim. The meeting soon came to an end, and I again offered him my heartfelt thanks for the opportunity to meet and for his timely, honest, and insightful counsel.

The imam worked his way gingerly down the uneven stairs of my office with the help of his two still-silent assistants, and I watched him with wonder. The instant he was gone, I turned to Ahmed, who was standing beside me, for affirmation of all that I had just heard. Since Ahmed is a Muslim colleague, the thought crossed my mind that he might disdain the imam's words and perhaps try to downplay them.

"Ahmed, please tell me, did I just hear what I thought I heard?"

But I need not have feared. I was still stunned and still shaking my head in wonder, but now that we were alone in the office, Ahmed's outward excitement surpassed my own.

"Monsieur Norman, I knew the imam thought highly of some of our work, but I never would have imagined he would say the things he did today. Is this not what World Vision is all about in Mauritania? Not only helping struggling communities to find direction and hope, but promoting tolerance and understanding between Muslims and Christians—values that are core beliefs of World Vision? This is what we have been working for!"

Ahmed's incredulity and delight surprised me. Here was a young Muslim man—a well-trained and qualified professional in his own right, but also a dedicated employee of World Vision— articulating his delight about the evident impact and role of an organization that was unapologetically Christian in an Islamic republic! At that moment I knew I would not need to tell, much less convince, our Muslim employees about the meeting with the imam. Ahmed would be sure his colleagues heard the story.

I spent the rest the day on the phone and drafting e-mails to all of our World Vision colleagues—our regional office, support offices, and international headquarters, as well as our international president, Dean Hirsch. I thanked them for their counsel and prayers during this time of difficult decisions, and I told them we were going to continue the work before us. World Vision's program in Mauritania would stay its course. The Holy Spirit had spoken to me with clarity through the words of an imam.

10

PRISON VISIT

Love your enemies, do good to those who hate you, bless
those who curse you, pray for those who mistreat you.
(LUKE 6:27–28)

IT WAS A RATHER HOT MONDAY AFTERNOON IN FEBRUARY WHEN
Amrita knocked on my door, stepped in, and asked if she could
have a word with me. Usually Amrita's entrance to my office
signaled something routine—a signature, a request for an appointment, or a gentle reminder to answer an item in my never-ending
backlog of correspondence. But her rare requests for "a word with
me" always signaled either a personal matter or something important that needed my attention.

I tried to read her face as she sat down in front of my desk.
Although a foreigner married to a Mauritanian, Amrita had a
remarkable network of connections, and her ear was usually

acutely tuned to all that was happening. Amrita explained that she had heard a bit of information about the assailant over the weekend that she thought I should know. She had heard it from a well-placed Mauritanian businessman in Nouakchott, a man I also knew personally. She suggested that she invite him to the office so that I could hear from him personally, which I readily agreed to do, knowing that Amrita's advice on such matters was usually worth following. The next day this man came by my office, and we caught up briefly about his work and other goings-on in the business world around Nouakchott, then plunged into the issue at hand. He said that there were some things I should probably know about Ali, the assailant, who was still incarcerated at the national prison.

Since the reenactment at the scene of the crime two months earlier, I had already had the opportunity to learn more about Ali. The police knew him, as he had had some previous run-ins with the law—smuggling contraband, drug trafficking, and the like. He was known as a lawless type and an occasional troublemaker who spent much of his shadowy life in and out of the country. He had managed to make his way back into town the night of the assault and hide for a few days before making his way south toward the border of Senegal. About a week later he was caught trying to leave Mauritania while crossing the Senegal River, which marks the border.

I had also learned that he was well educated and apparently had a military background but had been discharged for unacceptable conduct. He was also from a clan of noble heritage, the extended family of a traditional *emir* in the north of the country. His mother died when Ali was very young, and apparently his father had been a diplomat who had spent some time in Europe.

My business friend wanted me to know that, although our generous, public pardon for Ali would certainly help him, if and when his case came to sentencing, there was another matter we should be aware of. He had heard, through his own network of associates, that there were those who felt strongly that Ali's actions had brought intolerable shame to his clan and it was likely that, before his case came to trial, he would conveniently disappear. At first I was not sure I understood what I was hearing, so I pressed him for more explicit detail, and he reluctantly gave me an example. "For instance, you may one day hear that while being transferred from one prison to another, Ali perished in an unfortunate accident. And if you hear of something like this, you should not be surprised." I was shocked even at the thought. Now I understood why Amrita had felt so strongly that I needed to be made aware of this.

Later that evening I mentioned this news to Hélène, without the graphic detail, since Hannah was also at the table. But Hannah missed nothing and understood the situation much more clearly than I thought she would. Both she and Hélène were alarmed and appeared more disturbed than I was. There was a long and lively conversation at our table.

Hélène's first remark after absorbing the facts was, "We cannot let this happen!" And Hannah quickly echoed her sentiments with an ardor equal to her mother's. I sat across the table from the two of them, somewhat taken aback and after some hesitation defensively replied, "Well, what do you think I can do about it? It seems to be largely out of our hands!"

"But we must do something!" they both shot back.

Aboubacar, who had been quietly washing dishes in the adjacent kitchen, was aware that a heated discussion was going on. We communicated with him in French because he spoke virtually

no English, but he had been around us long enough to understand some. He was also keenly aware that most of the intense
discussions these days were related to the shooting and the host
of issues that came in its wake. Aboubacar was always reluctant to
interfere with our personal matters, but I knew he cared for us and
worried about our welfare deeply. We had also found him to be a
wonderful source of wisdom on matters concerning Mauritania.
As a Guinean, he too was a foreigner, but he had lived here many
years and knew the culture and customs much better than we did.

After a few moments we noticed that things were quiet in the
kitchen, and we realized that he had figured out, at least in part,
what we were discussing. As she often did when we faced difficult or complex matters related to local culture, Hélène decided we
needed to consult Aboubacar and called to him. When he stepped
into the dining room, dish towel still in hand, she filled him in on
the details of what we were facing, lest he had missed something,
and asked for his thoughts. In his quiet manner he said he understood that this was distressing for us, but that he did not find it
surprising. "This is the way things are here."

Later, as the discussion among the three of us continued and
as Aboubacar was assisting with clearing the dinner table, I could
tell he was taking in everything and was intrigued that Hélène and
Hannah felt so strongly about the need to do something. In many
ways I think this notion of concern for someone who had caused so
much harm was foreign to him. But he is a compassionate and merciful man, and this concern of ours obviously struck a chord in him.

Finally, after lengthy discussion, Hélène announced with an
air of finality that we would have to visit Ali in the prison and
take the matter from there. I then tried to explain to Hélène that
he was, without a doubt, prisoner number one in Mauritania, and

that it would be virtually impossible for even me to get approval to see him, much less take my wife along. Then Hannah, not missing a beat, interjected, "But I want to meet Mr. Ali too!" Her words silenced all of us. We stared at her for a moment, and finally I asked why she would want to meet the prisoner.

"Because I just want to meet the man who tried to kill you, Daddy. Besides, if you and Mom are going to see him, I want to go too!" Exasperated, I tried to bring reason back into the conversation. I retorted that there were absolutely no plans to go see the prisoner, hoping desperately to put the whole matter to rest. But later that night, as Hélène and I lay in bed, she told me in no uncertain terms that I must at least try to get permission for us to see him. I was exhausted from the emotional journey of the day, as well as the lively household debate that evening. But I knew when Hélène was on to something that I should listen. So I reluctantly promised to at least make an inquiry, then rolled over and tried to figure out how I was going to calm the tumbled thoughts in my head and get myself to sleep.

During the next couple of days, Hélène and Hannah continued to insist that we should try to get in to see Ali. I had hoped that within a day or two following the initial alarm this would subside, but I was mistaken. It was Hannah's persistence that surprised me the most. I was careful not to reinforce this notion by raising the matter myself, as neither Hélène nor I wanted Hannah to feel that we had expectations that she should want to do this. But whenever Hannah brought up the subject—"Daddy, are we going to see the prisoner?"—I always gently prodded to better understand why she wanted to see him. She would usually just shrug and say, "Because I want to." Hannah has always had a curiosity as large as the sky itself, especially about people, and so we just left it at that.

Hélène continued to feel a sense of urgency, so around mid-week I picked up the phone and made one of my routine calls to the director of National Security. After a few pleasantries I hesitantly told him I had an unusual request to make of him, and then asked if there was any chance my family and I would be able to get in to see Ali at the prison. There was a long silence on the end of the line, followed by a nervous chuckle.

"Monsieur Norman, I am not sure you understand. This man is not an ordinary prisoner, and neither are the circumstances that surround his incarceration. I do not think this will be at all possible." I knew the odds were impossibly stacked against such a request. I was well aware that the last thing the Mauritanian government wanted was any more troublesome publicity on the matter and that a visit to the prison by this American-French family would in all likelihood only attract the press. After a pause it seemed the director's curiosity got the better of him and he inquired, "But why in the world would you want to meet with him?"

My own reluctance in this whole matter was getting the better of me as well, especially since the director's short and clear response reflected the seeming ridiculousness of such a request. So I sheepishly responded that it was actually my wife and daughter who wanted this meeting, and I was simply following their request. The director probably thought I had a screw loose somewhere. This was one of the highest ranking men in the government of an Islamic state, and here I was on the phone making a halfhearted request on behalf of my wife and young daughter to meet with a man who at that time was probably the nation's most notorious prisoner, and a man the government probably wished would simply disappear.

But I stumbled forward anyway. "Well, you see, Monsieur le Directeur, this situation is tied to the healing and restoration process of my wife and daughter. Complex as it may seem, it would help them greatly to have a moment with the prisoner. Their purpose is not to accuse him or seek retribution, but rather to simply meet and understand better the man who brought such pain to their lives." Again there was a long silence. I have little doubt the director had never heard anything like this. But he was an intelligent man, and he was obviously absorbing what I had rather falteringly tried to explain.

"Well, Monsieur Norman, this is really a difficult request, and it is extremely unlikely we can make this happen, but given what you have said I will see what I can do."

We politely closed the conversation, but I saw that there was a sliver of a chance that this could happen, since I had obviously caught his attention. However, I also knew that if I did not persist with the request, it would be dismissed. So I picked up the phone again and called the head of security at the American embassy, a rather coarse and hard-edged man with a military and security background who had been involved in the case since the day of the shooting. I knew he had close contacts with the government's office of National Security, and I thought perhaps he could exert some influence. He was just as astonished as the director at what he considered to be a ludicrous request. But since his job, at least in part, was to represent American interests in Mauritania, and since he knew I was a personal friend of the ambassador, he took my request seriously, although he too indicated this meeting would probably never happen.

In the ensuing weeks, and often at Hélène's urging, I repeatedly left messages at both the Office of National Security and the US embassy, just to let them know that we were still persisting in our request.

The weeks and months passed by with little or no indication our request had been taken seriously. Life at home and within our World Vision programs was slowly returning to normal, although we all went through the motions of life with more caution than we had in years past. But our concern for Ali's situation continued, and at home we found ourselves praying for him and his safety from time to time, as there was little else we could do.

Then, late one morning, nearly three months after my first call to the director of National Security, his *directeur-adjoint* called to inform me that approval had been granted for us to see Ali in the prison. The only caveat was that the appointment was that day at 1:00 P.M. "Do you still want to meet with him?" was the final question. I stumbled out a surprised and hesitant yes, not knowing how this would go over with Hélène, much less Hannah, on such short notice. I had little doubt that our request had cycled through the highest echelons of the government and that the unexpected approval had probably come from the president himself. I learned later that staff members at the American embassy had also pushed the matter for us, crazy as some of them thought it was.

I grabbed the phone again and called Hélène. She was as surprised as me but determined as ever to make this happen. We agreed that I should call the school and explain the situation to the headmistress so that we could pick up Hannah, should she still want to participate.

When Hélène answered my phone call, she had been headed out to attend the small, monthly prayer meeting of mostly Protestant, expatriate women who met at the Catholic Church facilities across the street from our World Vision office. She told me she would go directly to the prayer meeting, tell her friends, and then meet me at the office within the hour. Hélène wanted to brief these women on what was happening so that they could be praying during our encounter. In the meantime I called Hannah's school and told them we would be coming by shortly to have a brief word with Hannah and possibly take her with us.

I had been instructed to meet some of the staff from the Office of National Security a little before 1:00 P.M., at which point staff from the US embassy would join us before we departed for the prison. It was a whirlwind moment, with little time to prepare our hearts, much less our thoughts. Hélène arrived at my office shortly; and after filling in Amrita (as well as receiving the welcomed assurance of her prayers), we jumped in the Land Cruiser and headed to Hannah's school. Since the time was short, I left Hélène in the car and found Hannah already waiting for me in the headmistress's office, a little wild-eyed but expectant.

I led her to a quiet corner in the lobby and gently explained to her that we had suddenly been granted a meeting with the prisoner that afternoon, but under no circumstances was she expected to join us if she did not wish to do so. A part of me was hoping Hannah would decline, but I also knew that she would be terribly upset had we not told her of the opportunity and given her the chance to go. I should not have been surprised when she eagerly affirmed her desire to go. I stared at her for a moment and said, "Hannah, you do not have to do this. Mom and I can do this, and it will be perfectly okay if you choose to stay here. And we will be glad to fill you in when we get back."

"No, Dad, I really want to go."

"You are sure about this?"

"Yes."

I gazed into her eyes for a long moment, trying to understand all that was going on in the head and heart of my young daughter, then resignedly said, "Okay then, let's go."

We drove quickly to the nearby US embassy and met up in front of the complex with the group of officials from the Office of National Security and those from the embassy. I stepped out of our vehicle and greeted everyone briefly. The Mauritanian officials were clearly in charge, and I noticed that several of them, as well as one or two of the embassy officials, were discretely armed. Obviously a little put out with this whole affair and in a tone that oozed sarcasm, my crusty embassy acquaintance leaned toward me and said, "I hope this is going to make you and your family happy." I thanked him for helping to make the meeting happen, which seemed to satisfy, at least in part, his apparent need for self-importance.

The *directeur-adjoint* made it clear that we were to follow his vehicle, and after arriving at the prison, we were to follow his instructions explicitly at every step of the process. With the Mauritanians in front and the embassy vehicle following, our convoy was soon winding southward through the hot, dusty streets toward the central prison.

We drove silently for a few minutes, each one in the vehicle busy and anxious with private thoughts about what would transpire shortly. But something about Hélène did not seem quite right. I glanced sideways and saw that she was sitting very primly, back erect, and staring straight ahead with hands folded in her lap. But under her folded hands on her lap was a plastic grocery bag filled with something. When I realized she was trying not to attract my attention, my focus soon zeroed in on the bag in her lap. She had noticed me staring at her as I drove, so I waited a moment, then inquired impassively about what was in the bag.

"Oh, I just thought I would bring along a few things for Ali."

I was now intrigued. "What sort of things?"

"Oh, just a few things I thought he could use."

"And what might they be?" I asked.

She reluctantly opened the bag and pulled out a few items. "I brought him a towel and a bar of soap, as well as a few magazines."

I saw the towel and soap, but then asked if I could see what magazines she had included. With growing exasperation she pulled out the magazines, and I saw they included *National Geographic* and a few other innocuous titles. But as I was still quietly pondering her evident unease, I noticed there was something else in the bag. As our convoy continued winding through Nouakchott's streets, and with Hannah intently watching the unfolding drama from the backseat, I asked, "Hélène, what else is in the bag?"

"Oh, nothing really."

"Hélène, there is something else in the bag. What else are you hoping to give to the prisoner?"

Soon Hélène let out a long, resigned sigh, and with a sheepish look on her face, she slowly pulled out the last item—a French Bible. I was thunderstruck!

With my rattled nerves, I was trying desperately to keep the vehicle on the road and not attract unnecessary attention from others in our solemn convoy. I hissed, as if the whole of Mauritania were trying to listen in, "Hélène! We don't even know if we'll be allowed to give him a towel and soap, much less magazines. But a BIBLE! It is illegal to give *any* Mauritanian a Bible, and you think you are going to march into that prison and quietly slip a Bible to the prisoner! If the authorities find out, and they surely will, we will be locked up with him! You cannot do this." She then threw a look at me that could have said I was the meanest person in the world.

"But he is such a hopeless man, and he so desperately needs to know that there is hope for someone in his circumstances!"

At that moment conflicting emotions surged through me, and I did not know whether to admire my wife for her incredible courage or scold her for her blatant foolishness. One thing was certain to me: I knew that I was neither as courageous nor as foolish as she. But this would simply not do. So, as Hannah continued to take it all in intently from her backseat perch, I begged Hélène to put the Bible away. And after a much-too-long period of silent contemplation, Hélène obediently slid the Bible from the sack on her lap just moments before our convoy rolled into the prison complex with a cloud of dust. My relief was almost unspeakable.

Before any of us could gather our wits about us, the others were filing out of their vehicles and motioning us to join them. We stepped out of the vehicle into the large, open space in front of the central prison. With another reminder to follow the *directeur-adjoint*'s instructions, I took Hannah's hand, and we were all soon plodding our way through the soft sand toward a large, formidable, and somewhat dilapidated-looking building complex encircled by a high wall. If one could imagine a building with cackling demons perched on its parapets, then surely this was one. It was no doubt one of their cherished strongholds in this land, and we were obviously about to set foot in their territory.

Although it was still midday, with a stiflingly hot, desert sun overhead, the prison gave off an ominous aura of darkness as we approached. As we neared the large, dark, solid-metal gate, Hannah's grasp on my hand tightened with each step—and with it my angst increased proportionally for her welfare. What were we doing, bringing our young daughter to such a place? Had we lost our minds? This was surely no place for a young girl. What seemed to be a grim smirk on the face of my embassy acquaintance as he glanced at our obvious and growing discomfort only served to reinforce my feelings of dread.

A member of our group banged on the metal gate, and a small, sliding view-hole slid open, revealing only the eyes of the guard on the other side. Our identities and purpose were given, followed by a short exchange in Arabic. The set of eyes disappeared as the view-hole slid shut. I confess that part of me yearned to be turned away so that we could return to our vehicle and get back to the normal routines of life—or as normal as they could be in the western Sahara. As I was pondering this appealing possibility, the huge metal gate suddenly began rumbling open, but only just wide enough for us to pass through one person at a time.

We filed across a dirty courtyard and were led by a turbaned guard to the dark doorway of the main building. As we were ushered in, out of the brilliant sunlight and into the dark, unlit interior, it took a moment for our eyes to adjust. But what struck my senses the most was not the sudden transition from light to dark; it was the stench—a stale odor of human sweat accentuated by the steamy heat that pervaded the building's unkempt interior. I was never under the illusion that a visit to a prison in this part of the world would be a pleasant experience, because I had been in others. But even my own sensitivities, which I considered to be well-rounded from years of living in challenging environments, were shaken. We were only seeing the public side, and I had little doubt there were other dark holes in the far reaches of this building that few, except their unfortunate residents, ever saw.

While my immediate concerns continued to be how my wife and daughter were taking this all in, my thoughts also turned to the many individuals who were relegated to conditions such as these for months and years of their lives. Granted, many were probably guilty of heinous crimes that called for justice and merited punishment. But even those individuals were created and loved by a merciful God, and how could a hole such as this provide the reform or hope so many of them surely needed? My heart ached from the sheer hopelessness and the aura of a dead-end chasm that this place exuded.

The director of the prison met our group and led us down a long hallway and into a rectangular room. Off to the side near the middle of the room was a battered table, and at the end farthest from the entrance was an old, metal bed frame against the wall, with nothing but a bare, dirty, worn foam-rubber pad lying on top of the failing suspension. Hélène, Hannah, and I were instructed to take our seats on the edge of the bed.

We were then told that the prisoner would be brought in momentarily and seated on a lone chair near the far entrance, and we would only be permitted a few minutes with him. At no point were we to leave our seats or approach the prisoner. But we would be permitted to address him from across the room. By this time the rest of our group had taken standing positions against the walls of the room, as there was virtually no other seating except for a chair at the table where the prison director sat surrounded by a handful of armed guards.

As the three of us sat there waiting for Ali to be brought from his cell, there was a cacophony of discussions, shouts, and orders going on in the now hot and crowded room. The noise grew over the next five minutes until there was a commotion near the entrance door, and a disheveled and confused-looking Ali was quickly ushered in and seated in the lone chair across the room. As soon as he took in his new surroundings and saw us seated at the far end, his face filled with shock and dismay. He had obviously not been briefed on the meeting, and his discomfort showed. He soon begged a cigarette off a nearby guard and, once it was lit, settled into what appeared to me to be a defensive posture. Somehow I had imagined that he would have at least been informed about our visit and our intentions, which did not include accusation or retribution. But one glance at him told me this was exactly what he was expecting.

By now the chaos in the room was reaching a peak. Hannah was staring wide-eyed at Ali, taking it all in. Hélène was doing much the same but also trying to keep Hannah reassured with her arm around her. Before things could get any worse and descend into chaos, I stood and with a raised hand and loud voice cried out, "Please! Please, everyone!"

I suppose my pleading surprised the crowd, and to my relief the noise in the room diminished considerably, so I turned to the director of the prison and asked if I could now address the prisoner. The director seemed to be relieved that someone was taking charge of the meeting and motioned with a nod for me to continue. As I turned to address Ali across the room, he stiffened, obviously bracing for a barrage of accusation or at least ridicule and denunciation. Within a matter of seconds the chaos in the room settled further, and one could have heard a pin drop by the time I spoke. No doubt curiosity was running high among both Mauritanians and embassy personnel as to what we were going to say.

"Monsieur Ali, first of all, I want you to know that we did not come here to accuse you nor to bring you grief. That is not our purpose. Please understand this. Rather, we came here because we simply wanted the opportunity to speak to you, especially my wife and daughter. It has of course been a challenging time for all of us, but your willingness to hear them and perhaps answer a question or two would serve to help us in this process. Would you be willing to do this?"

He was without a doubt relieved at my words, which had

seemed to ease some of the tension in the room, but I could see he still remained cautious and uncomfortable and continued to avoid eye contact as best he could. But with an attempted air of self-assurance and a tinge of haughtiness, he mumbled and shrugged his affirmation that we could address him and he would answer what questions he could. Of course, the truth was he had little choice in the matter. I had just wanted to make it a bit easier for him.

I then told the director of the prison that Hélène had brought some things for the prisoner. Hélène handed the plastic sack to one of the guards, and after the director briefly inspected its contents, it was passed on to Ali at the far end of the room. He eagerly looked at the contents and seemed pleased with the towel and soap, but he immediately began bartering with his guards to exchange the magazines for cigarettes. This restarted some of the earlier commotion, as a number of guards were obviously interested in the magazines. In a country as poor as this, current reading material was beyond the reach of many everyday citizens, so the colorful magazines quickly drew excitement and interest from the prison staff in the room.

In my continued attempt to keep some semblance of order, I quickly turned and took Hannah's hand, and as I drew her to stand next to me, I whispered, "Okay, Hannah. What would you like to say to Mr. Ali?" Hannah's standing next to me seemed to quiet everyone down again. Hannah was capable of expressing herself in French, but she was clearly anxious and leaned into my ear to quietly ask if I would translate for her. Up to this point, neither Hélène nor I had asked Hannah what she intended to say to this man. We had never wanted her to feel obligated to meet with him, much less address him. And I guess we had assumed that it was likely that in the end she would just come along and observe without offering a comment or question. So I was a little surprised when she came forward with her well-thought-out comments.

As I translated, Hannah began, "Mr. Ali, I have two things I would like to say. I want to ask you a question; then I have something else I'd like to say. First, I want to know why you tried to kill my daddy." The silence in the room was staggering. I admittedly felt awkward translating a question about myself, but I plunged forward with the translation. Had it not been a young, innocent girl asking him this question, I think he would have objected. He must have been intrigued by her spunk, because until this point he had avoided most eye contact with us. But I noticed that as Hannah spoke, he was watching and listening carefully. The question did take him aback, and he seemed not to know how to respond at first.

He shifted in his seat a few times and finally said with a sigh of resignation, "Ah! It was an awkward situation, a difficult time with all that was going on. Quite simply, I committed a huge act of gross stupidity." He then mumbled his way uncomfortably through a string of comments that were hard to follow, including how his foolish act had now put him in such a bad situation. But he eventually wound his way back to his earlier comment, concluding that it was just a stupid and foolish thing that he had done.

During his rambling response I noted that, unlike the time when we met at the scene of the crime, Ali never mentioned that his intention had been to rob us. To my surprise this was never mentioned during our entire encounter with him that day. And at no point in his answer did he tell Hannah that his intention had *not* been to kill her father, rather that he had "acted stupidly." As I tried to piece his thoughts and mumblings together, the impression he left me with (although he did not really say it explicitly, as it would only serve to strengthen the case against him) was that he had simply wanted to be a hero of sorts.

Hannah nodded that she had heard and accepted his answer to her question, so I turned to her for her next comment, translating as she spoke softly. "Well, Mr. Ali, I just want you to know that I do not have any bitterness in my heart against you for what you did, and I want you to know that I forgive you." I'm not sure who was stunned the most at Hannah's words. For Hélène and me, her words were a complete surprise. She had never articulated to us what she had intended to say, and we had certainly never coached her on what to do if and when she ever met her assailant. The others in the room, mostly a rough assortment of fairly hardened prison guards and security officials from various walks of life, were equally surprised. All eyes were darting back and forth between Hannah and Ali, without so much as a whisper. I could not help but shoot a quick glance at my friend, the crusty American security official from the embassy, to see his reaction, since his general take on all of this was that it was simply a foolhardy affair. He was standing there quietly, mouth agape and staring at Hannah; the look of tedium had vanished from his face and been replaced by one of intense curiosity.

As for Ali, his countenance changed noticeably, and it was clear to all of us that Hannah's simple words touched him deeply. He was no longer fidgeting in his seat and darting glances elsewhere, nor was he trying to barter any more cigarettes from his guards. He was staring directly at Hannah, trying to take in the words of this young, foreign girl who stood anxiously before him some thirty feet away. "Young lady, those are very generous words. I . . . I do not know what I can say."

I sat back down on the edge of the rickety bed with Hannah

and quickly turned to Hélène and nodded that this would be a good moment for her to share whatever thoughts she had. In a clear, strong voice my petite and usually demure wife leaned forward from her seat and said, "Mr. Ali, it seems to me you must have had a difficult life. To have inflicted the pain and suffering you did on my husband and daughter, surely you must be someone who has experienced a great deal of pain in your own life. Is this true?"

Ali stared at Hélène, nodding emphatically as she spoke these words, obviously amazed at her insight. Then he mumbled a few words about how hard his life had indeed been. She paused for a moment, then continued, "I don't know if you are able to read the newspapers here in the prison, but much has been said about how Allah surely protected my husband when the three shots you took at his head misfired. Have you seen these articles?"

He replied that he did get to read a paper from time to time and had seen some of the articles. He then shrugged and said, "Yes, I guess it is possible. Perhaps God was protecting your husband. I really do not know. It is really a matter beyond me."

In Islam, Allah is the one true God, who is almighty, omniscient, and requires obedience and unfailing allegiance. Yet for many (although there are exceptions), Allah is so great and exalted that he does not directly involve himself with the relatively insignificant affairs of most individuals. As such, the idea that Allah would *really* care or take intimate interest (much less intervene) with regard to the circumstances of an individual can be a foreign notion, and so Ali's uncertainty was understandable.

Hélène continued, "You see, Mr. Ali, this is what people have been saying, but I think perhaps something different may have been happening when the shots misfired. Have you ever considered that perhaps God was protecting you?"

This comment jolted Ali, as it did everyone else in the room.

"Yes, God cares about my husband," she continued, "and perhaps in some measure he did protect him. But I believe God's attention was perhaps focused primarily on *you* in the midst of this terrible event. Yes, your situation now is bad, but can you imagine the difficulty you would be in had you succeeded in killing my husband? You see, in God's eyes you are just as important to him and have just as much value as my husband. God's care and concern for your well-being extend just as much to you as they do to my husband and daughter! And I believe that God spared you because he still has a purpose for your life. There is still much you can do for good."

She paused for a moment, seemingly unperturbed by the absolute silence in the room brought on by her amazing insight. "There was once an acquaintance of Jesus called Peter, who felt so badly about himself and his past actions that he begged Jesus to stay away from him, saying, 'For I am an unclean man!' But Jesus calmed Peter, reassured him, and told him that he would use him for good to reach others. And because of Peter's acknowledgment of his fallen ways, God did restore and use him remarkably to impact many. In the same way, Mr. Ali, I believe God desires to still use you to impact others for good. You see, you are of priceless value to him, and that is why we came here, so that you would know this."

The utter stillness in the room was overwhelming, and everyone was astounded at Hélène's words, myself as much as anyone. I watched in stunned silence as the Holy Spirit imparted these incredible words of wisdom to my wife, who in turn poured them out with simple clarity to the man she had come to meet. In that moment I was witness to a fleeting glimpse of the incredible depth of God's love for all people. It took my breath away.

I saw in that moment that his love for the people his Son gave his life for is both stunning and magnificent, and that its depth is truly unfathomable. Sitting in that stifling, foul-smelling prison in a remote corner of the western Sahara—as Hélène continued to gently and boldly explain how a ransom, with a price beyond measure, had been paid for Ali—I witnessed the depths and wonder of that love and its stunning beauty as never before. And never before had I felt so humbled, privileged, and undeserving to be considered one of God's own and intimately acquainted with that love.

Hélène was now unequivocally in full charge of this meeting. But if her words had moved me deeply, her next action stunned me to my core. It was an act both frightening and courageous. As we were all still trying to come to grips with her remarkable words, she stood up from her seat. As she did so, she reached into her purse and, to my utter astonishment, pulled out a Bible—the same French Bible I had begged her to remove from the plastic bag she had prepared for Ali. She then strode quietly across the room and stood by his side. No one moved. No guard called out or moved to intercept her. She quietly opened the Scriptures, first to Isaiah, then to Romans. And for the next couple of minutes, as Ali attentively read along, she shared passages of forgiveness, redemption, and hope.

Although I was profoundly touched by this courageous act of Hélène's, I confess that I also felt the cold fingers of fear that had lurked constantly in the shadows of the room since we first set foot in it. And consequently, as my mind raced ahead of Hélène's words, it focused on the immediate consequences of her actions, not the eternal ones. I could not help but wonder if we would all end up in the same cell as Ali by the end of the day!

Hélène finished with the wonder-inducing words of Jesus found in John 3:16 and then told Ali if he ever had the opportunity to get his hands on a Bible he should read through the book of John, as there was much, much more to be found there. As she gently closed the Bible, my heart was racing uncontrollably and my eyes were fixed on the senior Mauritanian authorities in the room, desperately trying to read their faces and predict their response—reprimand and confiscation of the Bible at the very best, expulsion from the country or detention at the worst, although most likely something in between, I reasoned.

But Hélène was not finished. She leaned over to Ali and softly asked him if he would like to keep the Bible. *"Oui, Madame, bien sûr!"* As he said this he hastily took the Bible from her hands, lifted his blue robe, and placed it somewhere among his undergarments where, hopefully, no one would take it from him. He had rejected her magazines outright, but this was a book he obviously wished to keep. Without missing a beat, Hélène then swung around, locked her eyes on the director of the prison, and asked, "May this man keep this book?" The director, shaken from the seeming spell we had all been under, stiffened, then hastily nodded, *"Oui,* Madame, of course he may keep the book."

For the first time that day, I saw Ali smile.

Hélène was shaking almost uncontrollably, though imperceptibly to most, as she walked back across the room and took her seat next to Hannah and me. Then, to everyone's relief, with perhaps the sole exceptions of Ali and Hélène, the meeting was finally over. In an attempt to restore some semblance of officialdom and control, which had largely been dismissed (even shattered) in the last ten minutes, the prisoner was hustled out of the room—after which we were quickly escorted back out the prison gates and into the Sahara's staggeringly bright, afternoon sun.

Never before had I been so proud of or so upset with my

wife—and both in the same moment. As we drove back home, I feebly tried to remind her of the huge risk she had just taken. She silenced my protests with the words, "Well, I think I earned the right to do what I did, and it seems the authorities must have felt the same." Truer words could not have been spoken in that moment.

We had hoped that our willingness to forgive Ali in person, and our insistence on meeting him personally in the prison, would let the authorities know that we were following all that was happening with him and were interested in his well-being, even if he had been the one who committed such atrocities against us. We hoped this added attention would detract from any shadowy plans that might be in the making for his eventual demise. But more importantly, we hoped that in some small way our visit had brought a measure of comfort and reassurance for this man's troubled and confused heart.

The next day Hélène stopped by my office briefly for an errand. As we were chatting I noticed a large, black Mercedes-Benz pull up in front of the office, and a moment later a very elegant-looking Mauritanian woman stepped out and made her way to the reception area on the first floor. A short time later Amrita knocked at my door. When she stuck her head into my office, she informed me that I had a visitor.

Amrita maintained my calendar rigorously and faithfully rendered me the wonderful service of filtering out and prioritizing the plethora of visitors who wanted to see me for an endless string of needs. Usually an unscheduled visitor to my office would be quickly assessed by Amrita and either redirected to another staff member, or, if deemed important enough, Amrita would schedule an appointment with me for a later time. On rare occasions, however, Amrita would let me know that an unscheduled visitor was here to see me, and her knowing look made it clear that I needed to take the meeting. Such was the look on Amrita's face this time, and I knew she felt it important that I meet this person. Since the visitor was a woman, I was glad for Hélène's presence and asked her to stay with me for a moment until I better understood the purpose of this woman's visit.

She was a light-skinned, Arab woman in her late fifties, and she strode softly into the room wrapped in a beautiful, orange *malafa*. We greeted one another politely, although somewhat stiffly, as we were strangers; and as she took her seat, she removed her large, elegant sunglasses from her face. When we were all seated and facing one another, I leaned forward from my seat on the office couch and asked what I could do for her.

Her command of French was strong, and she began by apologizing for the unannounced meeting and thanking me for giving her a few moments of my time. She then continued, "You see, I am Ali's older sister. But since our mother died when Ali was still very young, I have essentially functioned as his surrogate mother all these years, as I am much older than he. I am granted a fifteen-minute visit with him once a month, and just this morning I visited with him. As I sat with him he began recounting your family's visit yesterday." Her voice began to trail off, and with shoulders shaking her eyes filled with tears, and she began to weep silently. Hélène and I glanced at each other and waited patiently with concern etched on our faces. After a pause, she continued, "As his account unfolded, he began to weep and was unable to continue for some time. So he drafted a letter in an attempt to express his feelings about your visit to the prison, and he asked that I deliver it to you." With trembling hands, she handed me a sealed envelope that Hélène and I opened and read together:

6 June 2002 at 9 A.M.

My dear little Hannah, Madam and Sir:

"The ways of Providence are impenetrable," said a philosopher in the 17th century. I cannot find the words to describe our meeting today. Although I still feel remorse with regard to the evil I have caused you, words cannot express the depth of my joy on Wednesday, 5 June 2002, in seeing you with your daughter, that little angel, alive and well! Madam, you demonstrated immense kindness.

The simple gesture of coming here illustrates, if there is a need to do so, a real nobility of feeling and the deep conviction in a certain understanding of the world. Many times I have heard of "Christian charity" (Christian kindness and love)— now I see it and experience it.

For me it is not sufficient to express my feelings of gratitude in traditional ways. In reality, this is a new path, which is opening up before me. This light which shows the way for what is "infinitely small," which I am, will end up transcending all obstacles which, until then kept me from what is "infinitely great."

Is this not an opportunity of which one dreams to prove to the cosmos (all that is) that all living beings can cohabit peacefully without any distinction of race, religion, or color?

Humbly, in a state of fallen nobility,

Ali Ould Sidi

When we finished the letter, we were visibly touched. Ali's sister then continued, "You are wonderful and kind people, and I cannot thank you enough for your generous act of kindness for my troubled brother. I know of no one else who would do such a thing for someone who had brought such harm to them." As she began to relax somewhat, she went on to express how dearly she cared for him. "He is like a son to me." She also explained that he had always been bright but had a history of psychological issues, was considered by many a social misfit, and had even struggled at times with drug abuse. Any one of these, I surmised, could have been the reason he was discharged from the military.

She clearly cared about her brother deeply and went on to express her frustration with the lack of help in a country such as Mauritania for someone with his challenges. Then, before leaving, she asked if by any chance he should ever get out of prison, could we, or perhaps our World Vision colleagues, assist her in finding a place, perhaps in Europe, that could provide help for someone such as him. She apologized for the boldness in such a request, but explained that other than herself, she had never met anyone else who believed there could be any promise for someone such as Ali.

—— 11 ——

THE LAST LETTER

When it was time to leave, we left
and continued on our way.
(ACTS 21:5)

GROWING UP IN AFRICA WITH MY MISSIONARY PARENTS AND
spending most of my adult life with my own family spread constantly over multiple continents, I learned that new adjustments
and changes are always lurking around the corner. It is just part
of the landscape. And as I progressed through these experiences, I
grew to be more malleable to the bends and contortions that this
migratory lifestyle threw at me. But one thing does not get easier
no matter how practiced I may be: saying farewell, sometimes permanently, to friends and relationships.

In the first fourteen years of our marriage, we had packed and
moved home and country at least six times. I well remember Hélène

sitting dejectedly among suitcases and boxes in our new yet moldy and roach-infested lodgings in Abidjan, Côte d'Ivoire, after just leaving our sparkling, clean surroundings of Oman. She lamented the pain of having left friends and community and contemplated the ominous challenge of starting anew: "It's like being stripped of everything, or constantly having your legs knocked out from under you just after you have begun to stand and walk!"

Listening to Hélène took me back to my own childhood years, when, after one of our three-year stints in Nigeria, we were ready to embark on the lengthy journey to the United States for our furlough—first by canoe for a day, then by Land Rover for another two, then by plane to Europe, and eventually another to the United States. We stood under waving palm trees on the banks of the Orashi River in the delta country of southern Nigeria as our Nigerian friends from the local community gathered around our family to offer a parting prayer and sing a tearful rendition of John Fawcett's beloved hymn penned in 1782.

> *Blest be the tie that binds*
> *Our hearts in Christian love;*
> *The fellowship of kindred mind*
> *Is like to that above.*
> *When we asunder part,*
> *It gives us inward pain;*
> *But we shall still be joined in heart,*
> *And hope to meet again.*

I looked up to see my mother dabbing her red eyes and hesitantly asked what was the matter. "Oh, Ray, the longer I live this life that I love so much, I've learned that the good-byes just never get any easier!"

That was forty years ago, and now I found myself living in the western Sahara Desert, still vividly remembering my mother's words I heard on the shores of that beautiful, tropical river, largely because my own life experiences, time and again, had proven them to be so true.

And so it was that in the spring of 2002 I began to sense another time for good-byes lurking uncomfortably in the shadows of my own thoughts. We still had concerns about Nathaniel being away at boarding school, now for his second year. For the most part we had been pleased with his experience there, but if we stayed in Mauritania he would need to finish out his high school years away from us. For all practical purposes we would never have him home full-time again. This worried Hélène. In addition, 2002 had brought some changes at his school, notably new house parents with whom Nathaniel struggled to connect, and some personnel were worried about Nathaniel's propensity to spend his free time with non-Christian and non-missionary youth, some of whom also attended the mission school.

Nathaniel was learning to be his own person, and we had a few concerns. But for the most part we had always encouraged our children to break out of the box and relate across cultures and faiths among their friends since we believed it would equip them to be more secure in themselves and have a better understanding of the world around them. In a few years Hannah would also grow out of her beloved school in Nouakchott, and her only realistic alternative would also be boarding school in Dakar.

I was also worried about Hélène, not only for the emotional toll of the past year, but also because of some chronic health issues that she had been dealing with long before the shooting. She had undergone surgery in Europe the previous summer, from which there were still repercussions, and getting good medical diagnosis and treatment for this and other ongoing health issues was difficult, if not impossible, in this part of the world.

As we gradually sorted through the issues at hand, it became increasingly clear that this season of our lives in Mauritania needed to come to a close in the not-too-distant future. Up to this point our children had never had the opportunity to sink roots in one of their home cultures for any significant period of time. The time was rapidly approaching that they would need to begin preparing to complete high school and enter their university studies. Hélène, more than anyone else, needed a break from running the homestead for years in lonely, challenging environments and a chance to sort out debilitating health issues that our stressful lifestyle had only exacerbated.

I agonized over this decision, and Hélène was a daily witness to my distress. Things were slowly returning to normal with World Vision's program in Mauritania, and our relationships with the communities we served and with the government, our principal partner, were as strong as ever. In spite of all we had been through, I was more fulfilled in my work than I had ever been. I loved the country, the people, and the work we did, difficult as it was, and my heart ached at the thought of leaving this all behind. What's more, I was loath to give the impression that our leaving, should it come to that, was a reaction to the tragic events that had taken place the previous year.

So with a heavy heart I began discussing with World Vision staff an eventual transfer, preferably to Europe or the United States. There was an opportunity at World Vision's office in Washington, DC, and I traveled there in the spring to review the position. A year earlier, and much to my surprise, Messiah College, a small,

Christian liberal arts college in central Pennsylvania, also had contacted me to gauge my interest in a forthcoming position as an academic dean. But at that time my heart was still fully engaged in my work abroad, and seeing myself more as a field practitioner, I simply could not envision myself in academic administration back in the United States. But during the time I was speaking with World Vision concerning a transfer to Washington, I learned that Messiah College had not filled the position and had renewed their search. I had my heart set on continuing with World Vision, but I had always known it never hurts to look broadly when making such a change. As my travels often took me to North America, and at Messiah's urging, I took a two-day detour during a visit to World Vision Canada to interview at the college, not really thinking they would want me in the end. Besides, I had told them that I would be unwilling to cut all professional ties with World Vision.

To my astonishment they offered me the position, with a contractual agreement that I could continue to serve in an advisory and consulting role with World Vision. Messiah College was looking, among other things, for someone to enhance their international ties and opportunities for students to engage more directly in service-related work.

When my family weighed in on the prospect of a more sedate academic life in suburban, semirural Pennsylvania versus fighting Washington's beltway traffic and having a father and husband who would be traveling the world 30 percent or more of his time, Messiah became more and more appealing. In the end I accepted the position and once more braced myself for another huge and somewhat daunting paradigm shift in my professional career.

I was now a seasoned mover, and I knew well the importance of ridding oneself of unnecessary and encumbering possessions that accumulate and being selective and discerning about the things to hold on to. But I had also learned the benefits of filtering out and registering in my heart important life lessons that a particular season in life had provided.

As our time approached to leave in the summer of 2002, I found myself looking back over our time in Mauritania, trying to piece together and capture the many valuable lessons we had learned in this remarkable season. I was keenly aware that Mauritania had provided us with an intimate perspective on the unfolding drama of God's unceasing care and love for all people that has been playing out for millennia. More specifically, we knew we had been granted a humbling, though tumultuous, view of the limitlessness of God's love for those we had been here to serve.

During walks with Hélène along the beach in our last months, not far from where our world had seemingly fallen apart the year before, I often thought of Sir Isaac Newton's reflections as he looked back over his remarkable career (as one of the most original and influential theorists of all time in the history of science): "I was like a boy playing on the seashore, and diverting myself now and then finding a smoother pebble or a prettier shell than ordinary, whilst the great ocean of truth lay all undiscovered before me." Newton was referring to the wonders of the created world and the natural laws that govern it. But the analogy can be expanded beyond the bounds of God's created order. I knew we had been given a small glimpse into something far larger than ourselves. God's love is surely boundless, and his ways with his people and those he seeks to draw to himself can simply not be foretold, much as we may try. And what we are privileged to hear and see in this lifetime, such as we did in our days in Mauritania, must be only whispers, encounters with just the "mere edges of His ways" (Job 26:14 NKJV).

During our time in Mauritania we had learned important lessons about prayer. First and simply, that God hears and heeds our prayers, especially when our petitions intersect with his heart's intentions and desires to bring hope to a hurting world. And we had learned that, try as we may, we can never presuppose his ways and the surprising means by which he may choose to answer those prayers. We had asked God to open doors of opportunity, and he had done so in a measure that far exceeded our expectations, but in ways we never could have expected nor ever would have chosen.

We had already learned the importance of being willing to receive love from those we were called to serve. In Mauritania we learned that such love can be God's manna-like provision of spiritual and emotional sustenance during wilderness sojourns, bringing healing and restoration, and to receive and partake of it with humility and open hearts. We had come to Mauritania knowing that God had given us a commandment to love, and we had come wanting to be vessels of that love in both word and deed. We were intimately acquainted with the limits of our own love and the importance of relying on a love that is truly beyond ourselves. But it was here that we learned that God's abundant provision of such love is unfailing, even in the darkest and most challenging of circumstances. After experiencing and surviving the horrors of the holocaust, then later encountering one of her past tormentors, Corrie Ten Boom framed it so simply, "When he tells us to love our enemies, he gives along with the command, the love itself."

We had also learned that obedience to this command means being vulnerable, and we had indeed experienced the hurt that can follow. At the same time we had also seen that in taking this risk, remarkable doors of opportunity could be opened to demonstrate to others the often-misunderstood nature of a caring God. This journey had brought us into a more intimate and priceless understanding of the One we had chosen to serve—an omnipotent God, who because of his love for us chose to be vulnerable, a choice revealed through the incarnation and demonstrated with humility, suffering, and eternal wonder on a Roman cross.

We had taken up our cross, perhaps clumsily, stumbled forward, and followed God to this land; but to our relief and wonder, we had encountered him most tangibly in the darkest and most challenging parts of that journey. We had *heard* his voice when he called us, but we found, time and again, that we *encountered* him most intimately in the places he had called us to.

Tired and extended as we were, in our hearts we had no regrets for having chosen this path. As Christians we often stand on the shore of the river of his love and observe with wonder its free-flowing and thirst-quenching journey through time and history. But God also compels us, as his people, to do more than just observe and offer prayers of gratitude and songs of praise for the wonders of his love. He invites us in. He invites us—even compels us—to engage and take the risk of submerging ourselves in its flow and releasing our will to it, as it then loosens our secure footholds and rushes us along well beyond our familiar surroundings to places and encounters yet unseen. And such had Mauritania been for us.

———•———

When we finally announced to our staff and friends that we would be leaving, we braced ourselves for the painful process of saying farewell to a country that had impacted us deeply and its people whom we had grown to love and cherish. There were many who had walked with us closely through the most challenging experience of our lives, and we were often at a loss to know how to say good-bye.

I made one last trip around the country to bid farewell to the communities where World Vision served, as well as to government officials and other partners in our work. During these encounters I tried to be transparent and explain the necessity for this transition in as simple terms as I could. But in spite of my efforts, there were still some among our Mauritanian friends who wondered if perhaps we had simply found life in Mauritania too harsh. There was no culpability implied in their wonderings, just regret, even shame, that their homeland could be so inhospitable for those who came to help; and I did my best to allay these reasoned suppositions.

It was particularly hard to say good-bye to our Mauritanian staff at World Vision. Many of them had given years of faithful service but had endured saying good-bye to their expatriate leadership much too often in years past—as most rotated in and out every three to five years. They hosted a traditional farewell meal, and as we sat under the large canopy of the Mauritanian tent, my colleagues shared many touching words of gratitude and encouragement. At one point someone mentioned the regret they felt that we would be leaving Mauritania with scars on our bodies. With my emotions running deep and threatening to overflow, I assured my colleagues that, truthfully, while Hannah and I would be leaving with scars on our bodies, there were none on our hearts.

About this same time there was a reception held in the courtyard at Nouakchott's finest hotel—a rather modest hotel by US standards, but the warm, collegial atmosphere of the gathering made up for any shortcomings of the venue. This evening reception was held to honor my family and me and to provide us the opportunity to say a formal farewell to our colleagues and partners in the Mauritanian government, various UN agencies and international NGOs, the World Food Program, and local embassies. It was a rich evening of warm exchanges and, for me, the sealing of many happy memories.

Toward the end of the evening, while my family and I were standing at the door shaking hands and bidding farewell to our guests, a senior official from one of the government ministries, dressed in a traditional flowing robe, approached and greeted Hélène and me warmly in impeccable French. Hannah had been standing dutifully and quietly beside us, and as guests passed by, she would on occasion get a nod or a friendly pat on the head as they left. But after greeting us, this official bent over and clasped Hannah's right hand in both of his. Hannah was a bit wide-eyed and self-conscious at the sudden attention. He gazed at her for a brief moment, then said, "Hannah! You are indeed a courageous young girl. We have all heard of your brave and selfless deeds this past year. And we are all sorry to see you and your family leave Mauritania. But please know, my dear Hannah, that you are our hero, and you will always be a part of Mauritanian history!" He gazed at her for another moment with a quiet smile of admiration, then turned and walked away as we watched silently, trying to grapple with these surprising and poignant words.

In the weeks just prior to our departure date in late June of 2002, Ali's dignified and elegant sister paid me another unexpected visit. She had only just learned we were leaving and seemed both alarmed and dismayed at the prospect of our permanently leaving Mauritania. Not quite understanding why she felt this way, I mumbled through a few reasons for our leaving and expressed my gratitude for her concerns, though I really did not fully understand what they were. She had been fumbling with the folds of her *malafa* in her lap with her eyes largely downcast up to this point—not an uncommon posture for Muslim women when addressing a male, non-family member.

When I finished rambling she looked up and squared her shoulders. Speaking softly but firmly she said, "Monsieur Norman, you need to understand that apart from myself, you and your family are the only people I know who care about my brother. He has no one else. And if you leave, I am the only one who remains in this country who cares for his well-being. You have exhibited great kindness toward him. And you and your family have gone beyond all expectations, beyond what I could have ever hoped for. But you are also the only hope I have for his future. When you leave, at best, he faces many long years of incarceration without help and without hope."

She paused for a moment and then sighed deeply, mustering the courage for what she would say next. "Monsieur Norman, I know what I am about to ask may seem foolish and presumptuous to someone who experienced what you did under the hands of my brother, and to someone who has already done so much. But would you be willing—and I beg you in God's name—to consider issuing a formal pardon to the authorities for Ali before you leave? It is the only hope he has to get released and have the chance of getting some sort of help. If you would do so, I promise you that he will do no more harm, and I assure you that I will do all I can to get him the help he needs. With the immense kindness and pardon he has already received from you and your family, I know that he desires, more than ever, to try to mend his ways. You see, I know him better than anyone else, and after what he has experienced in this past year, I am certain he will no longer be a danger to society."

I was very moved by her words, her courage, and her love for her brother, and I wondered if Ali knew what an amazing sister he had. In a society that can call for harsh justice for offences that shame family or fly in the face of cultural standards and expectations, even for family members, this woman's love for her deeply troubled brother was rich, genuine, and obviously ran deep. I pondered her request for a long moment as she sat quietly, obviously understanding my need to reflect carefully before offering a response. I knew that if the tables were turned, I too would be advocating for my own brother.

As I had done so many times in recent months, I quietly whispered a prayer for wisdom that I did not have. I cared for her and I cared for Ali. But as one who worked for an organization that had labored tirelessly for a healthier and safer society in this country for many years, I also knew that there were broader considerations. And I knew that I was not in a position to sufficiently vet them single-handedly. As I had needed to seek wisdom from the imam about continuing World Vision's program, I knew I would need to seek the wisdom of others on this matter. So when I finally replied to her, I explained as much. I also assured her that if I were in her place, I would be requesting the same, and I promised her that I would take her request seriously and seek the wisdom of my own Mauritanian staff in the matter.

There were only about two weeks remaining before we left the country, so the next morning I called our senior staff together. Two or three of our expatriate staff were present, but the meeting was primarily attended by our Mauritanian colleagues. I explained the details of my meeting with the assailant's sister and her plea for my assistance in obtaining a formal clemency for her troubled brother. I also explained that I felt this should be World Vision's decision, and that my response should not only be on behalf of myself and my family but on behalf of World Vision Mauritania as well. I had no idea how this would go over with my colleagues, but I was delighted when our expatriate staff quickly suggested that we defer to our Mauritanian colleagues on such a delicate matter.

I turned to them and asked for their thoughts. I knew they had all been impacted by our decision to return to Mauritania after the shooting, and especially the encouragement we had all received from my encounter with the imam. As Muslims working for a Christian organization in an Islamic republic, they lived with an understandable tension; and the events of the past year, challenging as they had been, had reinforced their belief that Christians and Muslims could work together on common ground for things we all believed deeply in—primarily improving the lives of children and their communities. Moreover, I had learned over the years through many personal conversations with each of them that they had also been deeply impacted by World Vision's core values—which are derived explicitly from biblical principles and which directly informed all that they did as World Vision employees.

Immediately several of our leaders spoke their thoughts.

"Mr. Norman, it seems to me that this request is in keeping with World Vision's values."

"Isn't this what World Vision is all about, promoting better understanding among people and advocating for tolerance between divisions of culture, race, and religion?"

"Our work is intimately tied to demonstrating compassion to those in need; why should we withhold it in this case?"

"I think by issuing such a formal declaration, World Vision Mauritania would send a powerful message to the government and to communities across the country about our core identity."

I was warmed by these thoughtful reflections, and soon the conversation moved to the more complex matters of examining the string of potential impacts (both negative and positive) such an action could have and the process by which such a declaration would be crafted and issued, since, to our knowledge, nothing like this had ever been done before. This was clearly new territory for all of us, but we were united in the decision that we should forge ahead.

By the end of the meeting, I asked three of our Mauritanian leaders to develop an initial draft of such a statement, and we also agreed that they would then confer with our lawyer (a local Mauritanian whom we kept on retainer) and vet the idea with some of our contacts among the judicial authorities in the government. The biggest challenge before us was time, as my departure was now less than two weeks away. Arranging meetings and working on an appropriate draft document in this environment could be agonizingly slow, but we needed to do this with as much local input and support as we could get.

A few days later they reported back to me. Although our lawyer and some of the authorities were surprised, if not taken aback, by the idea, they saw no reason why we could not move forward with it. And it seemed that as the deliberations continued, these individuals became increasingly intrigued and supportive of the idea. During my last week at the office, I reviewed a couple of draft statements, but the clock was ticking, and the process remained tied up with our lawyer and the time-consuming consultations in which he still needed to engage.

Our last day in Mauritania, and my last day as national director, arrived, and we were to fly out that night on the twice-weekly Air France flight. I was running between home and office, trying to wrap up things on both ends, and throughout the day I kept asking Amrita if she had heard anything. Word from our director for administrative affairs and our lawyer was that they were working frantically to have the document ready (and have the final green light from local authorities) for my signature before the close of business hours. That time came and went, and I had to get home for a shower and to gather up my family.

A few hours later we were at Nouakchott's small airport. My concern over the unsigned document was a blessing in disguise that helped to rein in my tattered emotions. I was about to leave a job that I had loved more than any before—and a continent that had given so much to me during a romance with its people, culture, and geography that had spanned more than forty years. And I was leaving it all for a new job and country that I felt I really knew little about.

Amrita, our faithful friend and co-laborer, joined us at the airport with all our travel documents in hand, along with about a dozen of our staff. To our surprise Aboubacar came into the small terminal with his sweet family in tow—all dressed in their finest apparel. Their unexpected appearance almost broke my heart and Hélène's, and I could see through his smile that Aboubacar was struggling as much as I with this moment.

In a short time our luggage was checked, and we had our boarding passes. As we were exchanging our last hugs and tears, one of our staff came rushing into the terminal waving a folder over his head. It contained the letter for which I had been waiting. Just moments before we had to board the plane, I hastily reviewed the final document, asked Amrita for a pen, and signed. Hélène herded the children toward the gate, and I turned and hoarsely offered my last *ma'a salama* (farewell) to my cherished friends. Minutes later the airliner lifted into the beautiful night skies as Mauritania fell silently into the darkness below.

The signing of this letter, drafted with the assistance of both Muslim and Christian, was my last official act in Mauritania. It was necessarily drafted with the rather stiff, legal terminology of the French language, but an approximate translation is as follows:

June, 2002
Nouakchott
DECLARATION

As my assignment in Mauritania is coming to closure, and in consideration of World Vision's founding values which advocate tolerance and favor-granting opportunities to people in hardship;

And because of the immediate support which my family and I received from the Administrative and Judiciary Authorities of Mauritania;

I wish to hereby inform you, on behalf of myself and my family, and on behalf of World Vision Mauritania, that we extend our pardon to Mr. Ali Ould Sidi for his extreme act of attempting to take the life of our daughter and myself.

In view of our desire to demonstrate compassion for the person concerned, and for his present circumstances and those of his family, we express our desire that he be given opportunity for sustainable reintegration to society in an appropriate manner, so that he may never again pose a danger to the public or be the source of future sorrow.

Since this matter regards the public, it is only the Public Prosecutor and his department—as he oversees all penal proceedings relating to such matters—who can bring these matters to closure.

Dr. W. Ray Norman
National Director
World Vision Mauritania

cc:

Department of State Security
Legal Counsel for World Vision Mauritania
Judge responsible for the dossier
United States Embassy
World Vision Mauritania files

When our plane landed in Washington, DC, no one was scheduled to meet us, so we knew we would be making our entry alone. It was probably better that way, since we each needed space in which to process this new and unfamiliar setting. We proceeded through immigration, collected our baggage, and soon found ourselves thrust into the bustling terminal and a new world of sights, smells, and sounds.

Nathaniel and Hannah were wide-eyed as they took in yet another new culture, and their stiff body postures and unconscious gawking at everything new betrayed them as true foreigners, the very thing they wished not to be. We paused momentarily in the midst of the commotion to redistribute the luggage among ourselves, and I asked Hannah to grab a particular bag. As I did so, I unconsciously spoke to her in French. Hannah instantly stiffened and hissed, "Dad! We are in America! Don't *ever* speak to me in French here. In America I only want to be known as an American!"

Hélène and I both stared at her in surprise. We knew Nathaniel and Hannah were excited to be in America, with the opportunity to live a normal life, whatever that was. And I knew that while Hélène would have the relief of not having to carve out a life in a remote outpost, she was keenly aware that America would still be foreign soil for her. But I had underestimated the youthful pressures and insecurities that weighed on each of our children—the gnawing desire to fit in and blend seamlessly into this new culture without the embarrassment of standing out like the awkward foreigners they were.

After renting a car we made our way north through Maryland and Pennsylvania toward our new home. The first hour was spent largely in silence as we each took everything in and processed it individually. Then we rounded another bend in the highway, and there looming before us was a huge billboard from a well-known restaurant chain with the bold words, "Eat, Shop, Relax!" We all gazed in silence for a moment, then simultaneously burst out in laughter as Hélène commented, "Well, welcome to America!"

We knew we were once again in a foreign land, facing a sign that beckoned us to take up a radically different lifestyle and a different set of values. As we rolled through the scenic rural landscape toward our new home in Grantham, Pennsylvania, my mind and heart struggled to make the adjustment. I knew I would need new strength and a new vision, and I beseeched God for such as I kept the car headed northward. I knew we were going to a place where the grass would be greener and the days pleasantly cooler, but I also knew that the stars would not shine with the same brilliance as in the land we had left behind.

THE STORY CONTINUES TO UNFOLD

And if you spend yourselves in behalf of the hungry
and satisfy the needs of the oppressed,
then your light will rise in the darkness,
and your night will become like the noonday.
(ISAIAH 58:10)

OVER THE YEARS, WHEN WE HAVE RECOUNTED THIS STORY, ONE OF
the responses we often hear is how courageous we were. My first
reaction is to recoil from such a suggestion, because as the events
unfolded none of us felt courageous. But this sentiment has caused
me to reflect more deeply on the nature of actions that elicit such
a response.

As for my family and me, I think many of our actions in
Mauritania flowed from our deep convictions rather than from
raw courage. And true courage seems to be inextricably linked to

heartfelt convictions. Convictions can be, and should be, intentionally developed and strengthened throughout one's lifetime. As Christians our convictions are understandably rooted in our understanding of Scripture. But convictions alone can serve little purpose when they do not inform the way we live our lives. Thomas Carlyle, the nineteenth-century philosopher who was raised in a strict Christian home and who later lost faith, surmised that "conviction is worthless unless it is converted into conduct."

How then are convictions effectively translated into action, and what fuels the courage to act on convictions? It seems to me that convictions come somewhat more easily than courage. Holding convictions generally involves little risk. The need for courage, on the other hand, implies that risk is afoot. But like love, courage flows best from the heart. We must ensure that our convictions reside in our hearts and not simply in our intellects, so that we will find the needed courage to act on our convictions, and to do so unwaveringly, wisely, and responsibly. Then we can do the otherwise impossible—forgive when it is unmerited and love across boundaries that are opaque and frightening. Courage rooted in our convictions, but which flows from the heart, begins to close the uncomfortable gaps we so often encounter between faith and intellect, and even holiness and compassion.

And so it was for us in Mauritania. We went there with the deep conviction that we were called to love and serve in the name of Christ—a mandate of Scripture for all those who seek to follow Jesus. In the midst of crisis, we may have appeared courageous. But our actions were simply our often-faltering attempts to follow Christ. They were a natural outflow from our hearts, troubled and hurting though they were at that time. But we were also the recipients of immeasurable acts of love and mercy by the One we have chosen to follow—and by other fellow followers we have been privileged to travel alongside in this remarkable journey of life.

My family's story is just a small subset of a greater and far more amazing story that has yet to reach its conclusion. The story of God's love—his reconciliation and redemption in the world and his wondrous, caring, and patient ways—is still unfolding. Our stories never really end. They keep going, just as the hand of a loving God never stops moving.

Summer 2004

It was only after our return to the United States that we as a family slowly began to put together all the pieces that compose the series of events recorded in this book. We found ourselves sharing bits and pieces of our story as they came to mind. But it took time for the whole picture to come together, even in our own minds and hearts. And I was hesitant to share portions of this story too broadly, due to its sensitive nature and the possibility of putting at risk World Vision's work or individuals with whom our lives had intersected in Mauritania, both Christian and Muslim.

I was particularly concerned about sharing the story of the imam's counsel, specifically in public venues such as church events. He had been generous and courageous with his words and counsel, and I was loath to put him in a potentially uncomfortable situation for the sake of an exciting story back here on American soil.

In the summer of 2004, I returned to Mauritania in an advisory role for World Vision's program development in new areas of the country. I was there for only a few days, and most of those were spent up-country. But I inquired about the possibility of obtaining an audience with the imam on the last day of my trip, when I would be back in Nouakchott. He was now Mauritania's chief cleric as the president of the Ulama, and obviously had an extremely busy schedule. No promises were made, but I was assured that my friends would make the appropriate inquires. I had no idea if I would be able to see him, or even if he remembered who I was.

Before leaving Nouakchott for our up-country trip, I had been hoping to see Ali's sister, and possibly Ali himself, but she had traveled to Nouadhibou, a northern coastal town. I was able to reach her by phone and inquire about Ali. I learned that Ali had eventually been released from prison because of our letter, and although there were some signs of progress, she indicated that he was still trying to integrate normally into society. "Ali still struggles, but you have touched his life and all of ours. You are good, good people. I cannot thank you enough." I was unable to see Ali—he had traveled earlier that week to a neighboring country—but I asked her to convey my greetings to him.

My few days in Mauritania soon came to an end, with no word about my request to see the imam. Then, at about 7:00 P.M. on the evening I was to catch a midnight flight, I received a call informing me that I had been granted a brief meeting at 8:00 that evening. A short time later a driver met me and took me through unknown parts of Nouakchott until we arrived at a large but modest home on a busy street. It was only then that I learned I was being taken to the imam's home.

Following proper etiquette I removed my shoes at the entrance and was shown into a dimly lit reception room filled only with a large floor carpet and a wide variety of Arabic and Islamic texts. The imam was sitting quietly on the floor in the middle of the room surrounded by a half dozen open texts. I noticed the individuals waiting on the imam showed him the utmost respect by their posture and behavior—kneeling as they handed him items and not turning their backs on him as they quietly exited the room. But I also noticed his graciousness and gentleness with these individuals.

As I entered the imam looked up, motioned me to take a seat, and said, "Ah, Monsieur Norman! And what matter brings you here?" We shook hands as I inquired if he remembered me. "Of course I remember you, Monsieur Norman. And how have you and your family been these past years?"

I gave him short updates on the family, then moved quickly to my reason for wanting to see him. "Sir, when we met some years ago, your words and counsel had a great impact on me, and largely as a result, World Vision continued its program in Mauritania during that difficult time. Since returning to the United States, I am often asked to speak to various groups—students, World Vision supporters, churches—about our experiences in Mauritania and among the Muslim people. Frequently I think about what you said to me and how meaningful your words could be to those I speak to. But I have not felt comfortable sharing that part of our story in public venues because I would not want to take advantage of your generosity or put you in an uncomfortable situation by discussing our meeting. In fact, I've often wondered if you remember the exact words you spoke to me that had such impact."

The imam had been listening to me intently. As soon as I paused with this last query, he did not miss a beat and immediately began speaking softly. "Of course I remember what I said. I urged you to do all you could to keep World Vision's programs going because of your love for the poor. I told you it was clear that you work with the poor because you love them, and our own people need to learn this. Monsieur Norman, I meant those words, and I have no problem with anyone hearing them. You are welcome to share them with any audience back in your home country, and if ever someone is doubtful that they are my words"—and at this point he reached into the folds of his robe and pulled out a business card—"show this to them." I took the card, printed in Arabic and French with his name and title, "President of the Ulama, Islamic Republic of Mauritania," along with his contact information.

He then went on to explain that he had recently returned from Madrid, Spain. Following the horrific train bombings carried out by Muslim extremists in March, he had been invited by the government to serve on an international panel to assist with national issues of reconciliation between Muslims and Christians. It was clear he was deeply disturbed by these acts by people who claimed the same faith as his. After sharing a few thoughts on his experience there, he gazed at me with sadness in his eyes and said, "Monsieur Norman, do you know what the real problem is with most people in our world today? Whether Muslim or Christian, so many people spend their lives with a spiritual void on the inside. They may carry external features, but there is a great emptiness internally." I could see hopeful longing as he sat there on the carpet surrounded by his many open texts and shared those profound words.

A short time later, as I was seated in the dark cabin of the Air France flight to Paris, I reflected for a long time on my encounter with the imam. His words of longing could have been from the lips of many a caring Christian leader I have known. Here was a man deeply and closely acquainted with truth—and I suspected he was closer to it than even I had dared imagine.

Summer 2011

After joining Messiah College I continued to serve in various ways with World Vision. For many years World Vision had been involved in the installation of boreholes, hand pumps, and sanitation facilities in rural villages across West Africa. One of my activities involved a multi-year study that explored issues of access and use of these water and sanitation facilities by people with disabilities. Once or twice a year I would take a small team of students to West Africa to assist with field research: to interview the disabled, test assistive technologies, and conduct workshops for World Vision personnel to help them better understand the needs of the disabled in the communities where they served.

In the summer of 2011, Hannah, who was studying at Eastern University, joined our student research team, serving primarily as a French-English interpreter for the other members of the all-women team. We were headed to Mali, a predominantly Muslim nation that borders Mauritania. I was thrilled Hannah would have this opportunity, as it would be her first time in ten years to return to the region of her childhood. My prayer was that this trip back to Africa would in some way serve to fully complete the circle we had begun pulling together when we chose to return to Mauritania after the shooting—that Hannah would feel fully at home in the land and among the people of her childhood.

When our plane landed in Bamako, Mali, late one May afternoon, I watched Hannah closely. I knew that in the next few hours her senses were going to be accosted by waves of familiar (and possibly overwhelming) sensations from her past—sights, smells, sounds, and the plethora of other chaotic impressions one encounters only in West Africa. Our group stepped out of the plane onto the small platform at the top of the open stairway, and the ninety-degree heat instantly assaulted us. Hannah seemed stunned at first, but almost instantly I saw the twinkle in her eyes grow as the memories of Africa washed over her: the smell of the dry desert air; the warm, jovial greetings in local dialects; and the broad, toothy smiles of West Africans among the growing crowd at the foot of the stairs. Hannah seemed like someone slowly waking from a long dream, as the reality of the distant past came flooding back to the present. When we paused momentarily on the platform, I leaned over and whispered in her ear, "Welcome home, Hannah." Without taking her eyes off the scene unfolding around her, she summoned one of her warm smiles just for me. It was a reassuring smile as wide as the sunset that was just spreading before us over the broad savanna plains.

After we had passed through the tedious immigration and customs formalities, we were ushered into the baggage claim area and the chaotic hustle and bustle that so often characterizes most West African airports: the African men in their smart, locally tailored suits engaging one another in friendly banter; the African women decked out in their colorful batik outfits and their towering headdresses barking loud orders to scrambling porters; and the sweating porters jostling for a preferred place along the hopelessly jumbled baggage conveyor. Hannah and the girls stood back quietly from the chaos, taking in the scene, while I jumped into the fracas to locate our bags. I had warned the other girls of this initiation rite to Africa, but they stood there with mouths agape at all the wonderful disorder and loud commotion. Hannah stood with the girls, but she was smiling knowingly, with her eyes darting to and fro, taking in all that was familiar in the chaos before her.

The half-hour ride to our hotel though the crowded and

bustling streets of Bamako was no different, with the other girls gazing quizzically at all that did not make sense, tossing questions among themselves and occasionally at me. Hannah's face was glued to the window, and it seemed to me as we wound through the hot, teeming streets of Bamako that she was quietly filling the void of ten years with the wonderfully familiar. That evening I went to bed feeling deeply grateful for how well her initial reentry to Africa seemed to have gone. I did not know then that the biggest test of this trip was still before her.

The next week flew by with the long journey by road up-country, stiflingly hot weather both day and night, long days in the villages interviewing the disabled, data collection at water pumps and sanitation facilities, and late evenings swatting mosquitoes and trying to compile our gathered information on our laptops under the flickering lights of the small World Vision guest house.

After a week the heat and long days had taken their toll on our team. We took Sunday off to rest and visit the open-air market in the nearby town. West African markets are an explosion of activity and a cacophony of sounds, sights, and smells that accost the senses in every way—the pressing crowd, the cries of hawkers, the bleating sheep and goats, and the smells of smoked fish and roasted meat, all rolled together in the stifling one-hundred-degree heat of the West African Sahel in May.

Around 11:00 A.M. our group of five stepped out of the Land Cruiser and headed toward the market. Just as we began weaving through one of the narrow corridors nestled between the thatched vendor stalls, I heard an unusual commotion only a short distance away. Passing some fifty feet before us was a small group of traditional minstrels and dancers surrounding a small group of men waving large rifles in the air. They were dressed in old animal skins, and I instantly recognized them as traditional hunters. They were obviously there for a local celebration, and I suggested to the girls they approach the festive hunters so that I could get a picture of them all together. Before any of them could answer, Hannah quickly declined and curtly declared that she would rather not involve herself with the hunters. Since the other girls generally took their cues from either Hannah or me in these unfamiliar settings, they hesitated; and we eventually followed Hannah as she deliberately moved down another market corridor away from the hunters.

From the look on Hannah's face, I instantly realized my mistake. The usual smile and inquisitive, discovering look in her eyes were gone. Her countenance was etched with concern and her demeanor somber and serious. I quickly moved alongside her and said, "Hannah, I am so sorry! I was not thinking!" This was undoubtedly the first time Hannah had seen a gun up close since she had confronted Ali's. Moreover, these guns were not in the hands of American policemen or deer hunters. They were in the hands of Muslim men in the same region where her world had been shattered some ten years earlier. The color was drained from Hannah's face, but she mumbled that she was okay and that she just wanted to keep moving.

Over the next few minutes we made our way slowly through the crowded corridor, but unknown to us the hunters had turned down the same route and were only paces behind us in the crowd. Then, like an unexpected clap of thunder, one of the hunters fired his gun into the air. Instantly the crowd cheered and the minstrels started up their music once again. But Hannah froze in her steps. When I moved in behind her, I saw her shoulders shaking, and it seemed she was having trouble breathing and was about to retch. I instantly drew her to me, and she buried her face in my chest. As she stood there quietly sobbing in my arms, I saw the large jagged scar from ten years ago exposed with each rasping heave of her chest. I held her shaking body closely and repeated over and over, "Hannah, hold on. It's going to be all right. Just hold on."

Hannah was determined not to make a scene there in the open market. As the tears began to flow freely down her cheeks, she quickly pulled down the large sunglasses perched on her head, gathered herself, and moved on down the corridor—struggling with every breath and desperately trying to regain her composure. She clearly hoped that by blending into the noisy, pressing market crowd, she would become invisible to it. The other girls knew something was wrong, but since they had not heard Hannah's full story, I am not sure they made the connection.

I walked alongside Hannah as she slowly took control of her ragged breathing and her tears. After a few minutes I turned to the girls behind me and whispered that we really needed to get Hannah back to the guesthouse. On the ten-minute drive back, Hannah was rigid and silent, staring blankly out the window. As soon as we pulled to a stop, she was out the Land Cruiser and into her room with the door quickly closed behind her.

I yearned with all that was in me to follow her into that room and hold my little girl. But another part of me knew that the girl who had just slipped behind the closed door was also a young adult who was struggling to cope with the brutally resurgent past as well as come to grips with her own future. I suspected Hannah needed to do this on her own. She was no doubt faced with her own human frailty, but she needed to find a way to summon her inner resources to surmount the confusion and leering fear that surely confronted her.

While giving Hannah her needed space, the rest of us sat on

the front patio of the guesthouse, quietly trying to occupy ourselves with reading or typing on our laptops. Every now and then one of us would steal a concerned glance at the closed door. Nearly an hour had passed before the door opened and Hannah stepped out. I will probably never fully know all that Hannah had to confront in that lonely hour; I can only imagine. But when she emerged I could tell she not only had emptied herself, but that there had been some sort of release and the matter was settled. She took a seat next to me, made eye contact and smiled, and then softly assured me that she was okay. Her color had begun to return, and there was a settled look of confidence in her countenance that seemed to say, "I can do this."

With Hannah's permission I turned to the other girls and said, "I think you need to hear the full story."

Spring 2013

In a country such as Mauritania, where the entire national budget does not even come close to that of many moderate-sized cities in the United States, government allocations for such things as social services are often minimal or nonexistent. As such, resources to assist the most marginalized and troubled individuals in society are limited at best. During the ten years that had passed since our leaving Mauritania, I had heard there was a quiet but unique and growing movement to help these individuals find ways to regain their sense of self-worth and develop meaningful and productive livelihoods. I had few details about this effort, other than it had developed significantly, was active in virtually every major township in the country, and was positively impacting many. The simple objective of this rehabilitation and social insertion ministry was to bring light and hope to some of the world's most forgotten individuals in a desperately rudimentary social services system in one of the world's poorest regions. It had gained significant favor and support from the government due to the quality and transformative nature of the service it rendered.

In the early spring of 2013, I received an unexpected call at my office. When I picked up the phone, the hollow, crackling sound instantly signaled the caller as one from distant shores. In a second or two I heard the voice of a longtime friend, Tom Abbe, whom I had not heard from for several years. Tom was a seasoned West African hand who hailed from Portland, Oregon, and who, after a long absence, had recently returned to Mauritania to work. Tom told me that earlier in the day he had had the opportunity to meet and have lunch with the man who oversaw this unique social services work, named Kamal. During their lunch meeting at a small café in Nouakchott, Tom had asked Kamal how this remarkable ministry had come about.

"Ray, you need to hear this story. What's more, Kamal has wanted to make contact with you for many years now and would welcome the opportunity to talk with you. May I put you in touch with him?"

The next day I placed a call to Kamal. He greeted me warmly and told me how delighted he was to finally have the opportunity to meet me, even if over the phone. He explained how he had always hoped to one day be able to thank me for the impact my family and I had made during our days in Mauritania, and to tell me how our own actions had deeply influenced the direction of his own work when he had first come to Mauritania. Kamal then began to tell me his story.

He had arrived in Nouakchott a short time after our departure, believing that God had led him there to serve but not really knowing exactly what he would do. He spent the first months learning about the country and culture but primarily praying about how and where God would have him serve.

One morning he got in his car and drove around the city, praying and seeking God's direction. He found himself driving past the national prison, and as he did so he noticed a Mauritanian man standing on the street with a small bag of belongings thumbing for a ride. Kamal did not generally pick up local hitchhikers, but he felt an unusual compulsion to give this particular man a ride.

The man thanked Kamal for his kindness and explained that he had just been released from the prison. He then told Kamal his name and paused for a moment. When Kamal did not react, he said, "You do not know who I am, do you?" As Kamal continued weaving through Nouakchott's confounding traffic, he shrugged and replied in the negative. "You see, I am Mr. Ali Ould Sidi, the man who shot the former World Vision director and his daughter. And today I have been released from prison because of a letter of pardon that Mr. Norman wrote for me."

This got Kamal's attention, but Ali was not finished. He gazed intently at Kamal for a moment, then blurted out, "You are a Christian, aren't you?" This second statement caught Kamal off guard even more than learning the man's identity. He hesitated for a moment before offering a cautiously mumbled reply in the affirmative. Ali continued, "You Christians seem to genuinely care about the neediest and most outcast in society, so you know what you people ought to be doing here in Mauritania?" Kamal kept silent with his eyes on the road, but Ali continued. "You need to help the many people like me who are society's throwaways. There are so many who lack a sense of personal worth and are hopeless. Such troubled men and women need help getting their feet on the ground and learning how to readjust to living productively in society! There is so much opportunity to help."

Ali paused briefly to gather his thoughts, and then he quietly continued, "Let me tell you what one Christian family did for me." Ali launched into the story of his encounter with our family when we visited him in the prison, the impact it had made on him, and the assistance we later provided for him to be released and have a fresh opportunity to try to sort out his tangled and disjointed life. Kamal listened spellbound to Ali's story, and by the time they reached the drop-off point for Ali, Kamal was sure he had heard from God about the direction he was to take.

Kamal began working with another man who had recently moved to Mauritania with his young family and who was already engaged in helping troubled individuals find ways to develop meaningful livelihoods in the Nouakchott area. Some time later, Kamal's colleague was tragically assassinated on the streets of Nouakchott. This was, of course, a huge setback, but with continued encouragement from local authorities, Kamal took over the work and has seen it grow and flourish in the years that have followed.

Kamal went on to say that he and Ali became friends, and for several years they met frequently, often with Kamal providing counsel and assistance to Ali as he struggled to reintegrate into society. He mentioned that Ali continued to have both high and low points in his life as he dealt with his troubled past and his own psychological challenges before passing away in 2012.

"But, Mr. Norman," Kamal said at last, "I have always wanted you to know what a profound impact you and your family had on Ali and how grateful he always was for what you did for him. God has blessed our ministry in remarkable ways. We are now working in virtually every major city and town in Mauritania, assisting hundreds of broken lives, and much of our work is where it is today because of the testimony of Ali and my encounter with his desire to help others who have traversed the same difficult path as he."

When I got off the phone with Kamal, I called Hannah in her dorm room at Eastern University and told her the story I had just heard. Then I quietly told her that Ali had passed away in 2012. At first there was a long silence on the other end of the line. Then Hannah began to weep. She wept for a long time, as anyone would who had lost someone whom they cared about deeply.

AUTHOR'S NOTE AND ACKNOWLEDGMENTS

THE RECOUNTING OF THIS STORY MORE THAN TEN YEARS AFTER THE events has been a unique journey for my family and me. At times it has been heartwarming, but at other times it has been tumultuous, even quite painful – especially when confronted by both our past and continuing frailties and shortcomings. During the events recounted, we were often blind to the bigger picture of all that was happening. And in the midst of the turmoil we simply tried to make it through each day intact, hoping to at least "stumble forward" with each step we took. But as the years progressed we were able to gradually process and piece together the full story recorded in this book. As the pieces came together, we discovered that the *way* in which we remember and process the events in our lives may often be far more significant than simply the events themselves. Henri Nouwen, in his little book *The Living Reminder*, framed this so well: "Our memory plays a central role in our sense of being, [and] the events of our lives are probably less important than the form they take in the totality of our story . . . Our first and most spontaneous response to our undesirable memories is to forget them . . . [But] by refusing to face our painful memories we miss the opportunity to change our hearts and grow mature in repentance." Our hearts have certainly been stretched, changed, and hopefully enlarged. And we have been humbled in the process as we have seen how God's hand was over it all along. It is my hope that readers will find that the journey of our hearts has also been as faithfully recorded as the events themselves.

As I penned this narrative, I did so hesitantly, feeling neither competent nor worthy of the task. I felt this way for a number of reasons. First, in my heart, I am intimately aware that I am no hero or one endowed with particular spiritual insight or strength, as is the rest of my family – a notion that seems to be rather uncomfortably attached to us when have recounted this story in part or in whole. I have felt this way especially when I compare myself to many other followers of Jesus my own journey has privileged me to intersect with. Secondly, I am a water engineer and an international development practitioner. I am not a theologian or a Muslim scholar. And my experience of writing has largely been in the academic fields and not for the general public. Thirdly, I have written about experiences which occurred while living and working among some of the world's most disadvantaged and vulnerable people. I do not and cannot write from their perspective, much as I wish or would like to think I could. Rather, I have written from the limited (and disadvantaged) vantage point of a person with incredible privilege in today's world. I am a white male, a citizen of both the United States and France, and while writing this book I worked as an academic at a respected, private institution of higher learning—an institution that is also beyond the means of most people my life has intersected with.

My primary consolation when wrestling with these conflicted feelings, is that I have had the wonderful privilege of spending much of my lifetime (and its happiest moments) walking alongside—in their farms, homesteads and villages—many who have not had the worldly privileges I have had. This experience has shaped me deeply, especially in my understanding of myself and the gospel. I was also raised by parents who were deeply committed to the cause of Christ in a broken and hurting world, and who always held an abiding love for the poor and disadvantaged, a love that deeply informed most every aspect of their lives, whether during their many years serving as missionaries in Africa, or as a medical doctor and English teacher in the U.S. And, I have had a wonderful, lifelong companion and wife who has shared my own heart for a broken world and has always been there to faithfully remind and prod me to do the "right thing" whether I have felt qualified or not—such as write this book.

I also owe much to my two children, Nathaniel and Hannah, who traversed, with exceptional grace and patience, a veritable kaleidoscope of experiences as their mom and dad dragged them across multiple continents and cultures in their growing-up years. I am also indebted to my sister, Jo Ellen—who prayed faithfully for us during our years abroad and who diligently handled many of our logistics back in the U.S; and to my brother, Russell, who in the midst of his own busy life would on occasion send a word of encouragement my way—encouragement that I would hold on to like a jewel. And to my European in-laws, Pierre and Janet Derchez, who have bravely stepped across the cultural divide these many years and loved and accepted me as one of their own.

In getting to the point of actually writing this story, there are others I am deeply indebted to. My many friends and colleagues at World Vision—Dave Robinson, Rich Stearns, Daniel Ole Shani, Mekonnen Sisay, Larry Probus, Jean-Baptiste Kamate, Torrey Olsen, and Chawkat Moucarry to name only a few who encouraged this endeavor. Dave Robinson's wise and consistent counsel through the years to "share your important story" has been a huge source of inspiration and encouragement. And I owe especial thanks to Rich Stearns, who more than anyone else, encouraged, prodded and motivated me to actually sit down and put pen to paper. I am also grateful to Messiah College, which provided a rich environment for exchange and reflection, to its leadership who granted me a four-month leave-of-absence to get this work underway, and to my Messiah College colleagues who over the years have encouraged us to share our story more broadly: the late Terry Earhart, Theodore and Cathy Prescott, Michael Cosby and Angela Hare, among others. And elsewhere, there have been other friends and acquaintances who have provided invaluable encouragement and assistance to this endeavor: Dennis Hollinger, Steve Bundy, Joni Eareckson Tada, Stan and Beth Doerr, Mike Leonzo, David Shenk and Lori Zimmerman, especially.

In the early stages of writing I received invaluable editorial guidance and assistance from Becky Kaspareck and Lynne Cosby. My agent, Bill Denzel, shepherded me wisely through the initial phases of putting a book together, and my editors at Thomas Nelson, Webster Younce, Heather Skelton, and Kristen Parrish provided me with much needed advice and encouragement as they patiently guided me through the final steps.

Lastly, as I penned this story, I wrestled frequently with understanding and articulating the parallel, internal journey of my own heart. In re-crossing this daunting landscape, and in the unpacking of a confusing mix of past memories, emotions, and convictions, I was often compelled to call upon the only one who has been there to accompany me through each step (and misstep) for wisdom and guidance. And it is to him I owe everything: Isa al-Masih (Jesus the Messiah), who has liberally given me all I have yearned for—truth to satisfy my intellect, love to fill my heart, and, always, bright hope for the future.

ABOUT THE AUTHOR

RAY NORMAN WAS RAISED IN RURAL WEST AFRICA, THE SON OF medical missionaries. After completing his formal education, he worked in Africa and the Middle East for more than fifteen years as a researcher and development specialist in the water and agricultural sectors—serving with Cornell University (Niger), Winrock International (Niger), Sultan Qaboos University (Oman) and the African Development Bank (Côte d'Ivoire and Egypt). During this time his work was focused primarily on the socio-technical interface between traditional societies and water use. In 1999 he joined World Vision International as the national director in the Islamic Republic of Mauritania. After serving with World Vision, Ray and his family returned to the United States so their children could complete their education. He served as dean of the School of Science, Engineering, and Health at Messiah College for some twelve years, while continuing to intersect with World Vision in an advisory and consulting capacity. Over the years, he has also worked as a consultant to the US Agency for International Development, the World Bank, the Millennium Challenge Corporation, and various international NGOs—largely as an irrigation and water management specialist. He returned to World Vision in 2015 as the director for Faith Leadership for their global Water, Sanitation, and Hygiene programs. He also speaks frequently at both professional conferences and church-related venues on issues of international development, poverty reduction, cross-cultural relations, and Christian witness. Ray holds a PhD in Agricultural and Biological Engineering from Cornell University. He is married to Hélène (a French national) and has two grown children, Nathaniel and Hannah. They divide their non-traveling time between the villages of Grantham, Pennsylvania, and Bonningues-les-Ardres in northern France and are members of Living Water Community Church in Harrisburg, Pennsylvania—an inner-city, multi-ethnic church that works to bring justice and hope to the urban communities it serves.